ISHI MEANS MAN
Essays On Native Americans

THOMAS MERTON

ISHI
MEANS
MAN

Foreword by Dorothy Day
Woodblock by Rita Corbin

Unicorn Press, Inc.
Greensboro, North Carolina

Grateful acknowledgement is made to the editors of *The Catholic Worker, The Center Magazine, Theoria to Theory, Unicorn Journal*, in which these essays first appeared.

The editor is indebted to Brother Patrick Hart, O.C.S.O., of The Abbey of Gethsemani, to James Laughlin, and to Naomi Burton Stone for editorial assistance.

LC Number 75-12192
ISB Number 0-87775-074-2, paper
ISB Number 0-87775-100-5, cloth

The Unicorn Keepsake Series, edited by Teo Savory and designed by Alan Brilliant, is published by Unicorn Press, Inc., P.O. Box 3307, Greensboro, North Carolina 27402.

Table of Contents

Foreword by Dorothy Day

PART I

The Shoshoneans / 5
War and Vision / 17
Ishi: A Meditation / 25

PART II

The Cross-Fighters / 35

The Sacred City / 53

FOREWORD

R EADING AGAIN THESE ESSAYS, some of which we are proud
to have printed in *The Catholic Worker,* I could only
cry out, as another staff member did, "More, more!"

One feels a great sense of guilt at knowing so little about
the Indians of the Americas. As children, when we played the
game of Indians and cowboys, it was always the Indians who
were the aggressors, the villains. And then in my late teens I
read an account of the Jesuits among the Indians in upper
New York state and in Canada, and remembered only the tortures undergone by the missionaries. In our history books the
French and Indian wars only confirmed our idea that the Indians were enemies. We quite forgot the story of our earliest
colonists and the aid the Indians had given them, teaching
them how to survive in what was, to them, a harsh and barren
land, during those first winters.

Only John Collier's book on the Indians of the Americas,
printed first in the Forties, more than a generation ago, brought
me out of my abysmal ignorance. That book had far-reaching
influence, as I hope this book of essays will have. Only recently
an English editor, John Papworth, called upon by the presi-
dent of Zambia, Kenneth Kaunda, to be an adviser to his
small African state (next door, one may say, to Tanzania and
its brilliant leader, Julius Nyerere), confessed that the book
which had led him to a deep interest in primitive cultures and
all they could teach us, was that by John Collier. I'm hoping
that Unicorn Press will be deluged with orders for this inspiring collection of Merton's essays.

We owe a debt of gratitude to Thomas Merton, Trappist
monk and scholar, and to Unicorn Press for gathering these
writings together.

Dorothy Day

PART I

THE SHOSHONEANS

Indians who are now principally on the reservation were the aboriginal owners of the United States. Placing them on reservations was an act to protect the white settlers from acts of depredation, which became more common as the Indians were pushed further back out of their original holdings.
From a Government Mimeographed Sheet about the Indians of Fort Hill Reservation, Idaho

THE ABOVE STATEMENT, the modest production of some very minor bureaucratic mind, merits our attention. Indeed it merits more than that: perhaps an international prize for crass and impenetrable complacency. But at any rate, failing an international prize, our attention. "Indians," it says. The subject of the mimeographed sheet is Indians. What are Indians? Everybody and nobody knows what are Indians, but anyhow they are "principally" (let us not get into exquisite details) they are "principally" on "reservations." In point of fact, once it is imagined that you know who they are, it is enough to remember also where they are. The "where" is an extension of the "who." That is to say, you can guess who the Indians are by viewing them in the world of essences which is TV. And the "where" follows as an obvious conclusion. They are "principally on reservations" since they are essentially people who have to be punished for shooting at covered wagons. Why "principally?" They do not have to stay on reservations. They have other choices: to bite the dust or move elsewhere—for example to a ghetto in Reno. Or even to Brooklyn, for that matter. But they live principally on reservations where they are, as we might expect, "shiftless." They do not "take responsibility," since they are Indians. Like certain other races, they seem to gravitate to "run down sections." They are also considered "minors," you know, "wards of the government."

5

Incidentally, in passing, they did once in a manner of speaking qualify as "property owners," but of course only in a very mystical, primitive, irresponsible way, a way utterly laughable. They seemed to be owners of the whole continent, until we arrived and informed them of the true situation. They were squatters on land which God had assigned to us. We knew immediately, we could see at a glance, we understood without the slightest hesitation, that they were only *aboriginal* owners. Now you know and I know just how much of an owner that is. Really no owner at all. The Indian had all this real estate but never even knew it was real estate. So he never really had any legal title. He never even *claimed* a legal title. What a betrayal of responsibility! What shameful disrespect for the basic value of life: property ownership! The aboriginal owner was content to put forward some fantastic story about ancestors, about living here, about having the right to hunt in order to stay alive, and other romantic nonsense. From the first it was quite evident that the manifest destiny of the Indian was to live "principally" on reservations as wards of the true owners of the land, the ones for whom legal title had been prepared in some mysterious fashion from the beginning of time, or drawn up perhaps in Noah's ark.

So we magnanimously shouldered our responsibility for this great continent. In so doing we also shouldered the aboriginal owners and placed them (with the help of the military) principally on reservations appropriate for the irresponsible— that is to say tracts of land that were already remote and a bit run down.

Remember: there were always those "depredations." The sort of thing a sneaky old aboriginal owner might resort to. Just when the white man is starting to develop the neighborhood, to make a little money on his investment, along come the Indians with their depredations, stealing horses for example, not only in order to ride them but even in some deplorable cases to eat them, hunger being one of the weaknesses of aboriginal owners who suddenly learn that they are no longer in a position to live by hunting, since the white man has destroyed all the game.

In 1965 Edward Dorn, a poet, and Leroy Lucas, a photographer, went looking for the Shoshonean Indians, in the Basin Plateau, the high, dry, valleys of Nevada and Idaho. Their itinerary took them from Reno to the Paiute reservation around Pyramid Lake, to the Western Shoshoni at Duck Valley on the Nevada-Idaho border, to the Shoshoni-Bannock at Fort Hall reservation in the Snake River valley of Idaho. They wanted something more than to "see" these people, these "aboriginal owners" long since separated from their "original holdings" and reduced to a state of alienated helplessness. They did not simply come to point a camera at human objects and make notes about the folkways of a distraught minority. In their book,* Dorn's text does not even pretend to be sociology and the eye of Leroy Lucas's camera discovers images strangely unlike what we might find in the *National Geographic*. These are not the photographs which somehow manage to ignore Indians and treat them as if they weren't there—making them disappear in a raw, post-card colored landscape and an incomprehensible costume. The aboriginal owner has a face marked with suffering, irony, courage, sometimes desperation: always with a human beauty which defeats sometimes obvious degradation. Perhaps the explanation for this clear vision is the fact that Lucas is a Negro and knows what he is seeing when he looks at people who have been systematically excluded from life, and who yet manage to remain very much alive, at once present and lost, accusingly separate and outside. Yet very much "there."

The journey of Dorn and Lucas was a pilgrimage. What is a pilgrimage? A journey to the source, a return to a place where there will be an encounter and a renewal of life. The beauty of this book is precisely in this pilgrimage aspect; it is not a sentimental journey into a romantic past, but a humble,

*The Shoshoneans by Edward Dorn, photographs by Leroy Lucas. (William Morrow, New York, 1967)

difficult, necessarily incomplete effort to cross an abyss and achieve communion with people who, in such large measure deprived of identity and reduced to inarticulate silence, have little or nothing left to say in ordinary language. Dorn highlights this pilgrimage theme by devoting the first chapter to a hundred-and-two-year-old Indian, "probably the oldest living being in Idaho or Nevada," whom he visited one hot afternoon in a dirty little shack. Description of the mess in the old man's room. Description of his look: *"Very old animals have such coats over the eyes, a privacy impenetrable from the outside."* Yet even then an overpowering "presence" and with it all the appalling neglect of a life burned out finally after a hundred years of poverty, a "man gone to the utter end." Attempts to communicate: did the old Father need anything? Finally they discover that he likes cigarettes. They leave him with several cartons. They hope the mysterious smile of a passer-by is a sign that communion now exists.

The whole book is pitched low like this. Nothing is romanticized. The life of the "aboriginal owner now principally on reservations" is hardly touched by glamor. There is a pitiful beauty in it, but the squalor in which the beauty persists is not evaded or drenched in nostalgia. The book is quietly eloquent, objective, without camouflage, confessedly incomplete and tentative. It is an attempted pilgrimage to the point "beyond which there would lie the fullest explanation of a people who have been so fully maligned by crimes of omission." The authors have the honesty to admit that they never reached any such point. But the photographs and text give us a valid idea of what that point might be.

What about the Shoshoneans and the United States of America? Indians who have fought in the "Korean conflict." Indians who like war. Ritual flag raising incorporated into the Sun Dance. But also: the Sun Dance for Peace in Vietnam. Leroy Lucas, the Negro, participated in the Sun Dance, danced for the full three days, fasting, in the hot sun. Fine pictures give some idea of the dance but it is only alluded to, in passing, by Dorn's text. Dorn was not there.

Meanwhile Radio KSSN, Pocatello, Idaho, praised, if not the Sun Dance for peace, at any rate a War Dance for War: "Congratulations out there all you Shoshoni Bannocks for a job well done, and all you Shoshoni Bannocks participating out there at Fort Hall, Ross Fork an' Tyhee . . . We can all be proud of the war dancers." Sure, a war dance is safe enough now it no longer means anything. That is why we can be proud of it. We are indeed proud of our Indian friends. They have accepted their meaninglessness.

Or have they?

What do they make of themselves "out there" on the reservation?

Are they simply content to believe what we have made of them?

The precise question must be clearly defined. Let us return to the original statement, from the mimeograph about Fort Hall. The Indian has been forcibly confined within the limits of a mental definition that is at once arbitrary and unlivable. Of this, his existence on the reservation (principally), as a minor and ward of our government, as a being who is assumed to be unable to decide anything for himself, is only a symbolic, ritual expression. The real confinement, the real reduction and unmanning of the Indian is the reduction to a definition of him not in terms of his essential identity, but purely and simply in terms of his relations with us. More exactly, a definition of him in terms of a relationship of absolute tutelage imposed on him by us. This is of course extremely significant not only for the Indian (against whose human identity it is an act of systematic violence) but for ourselves.

In defining and limiting the Indian as we have, we are also expressing a definition and limitation within ourselves. In putting the Indian under tutelage to our own supposedly superior generosity and intelligence, we are in fact defining our own inhumanity, our own insensitivity, our own blindness to human values. In effect, how is the Indian defined and hemmed in by the relationship we have imposed on him? His reservation existence—somewhat like the existence of an orphan in an asylum—is as close to non-existence as we can get him without annihilating him altogether. I fully realize that this will arouse instant protest. The Indian is not confined to his reservation: he has another choice. He is free to raise himself up, to get out and improve his lot, to make himself human, and how? Why, of course, by joining us, by doing as we do, by manifesting business acumen and American knowhow, by making money, and by being integrated into our affluent society. Very generous indeed.

But let us spell out quite clearly what this means. IT MEANS THAT AS FAR AS WE ARE CONCERNED THE INDIAN (LIKE THE NEGRO, THE ASIAN, ETC.) IS PERMITTED TO HAVE A HUMAN IDENTITY ONLY IN SO FAR AS HE CONFORMS TO OURSELVES AND TAKES UPON HIMSELF OUR IDENTITY. But since in fact the Indian, or the Negro, is in the position of having a different colored skin and other traits which make him unlike ourselves, he can never be like us and can therefore never have an identity. The lock snaps shut. The Indian, like the Negro (though perhaps less emphatically), is definitively excluded. He can never sell himself to us as fully human on our impossible terms. In theory we recognize his humanity. In practice he is, like the Negro, at best a second-class human who tries to dress and act like ourselves but never quite manages to make the grade. Therefore "Indians are now principally on the reservation." They have failed to establish themselves in our society, "But," and we continue to paraphrase, "placing them on reservations was an act to protect white settlers from psychological depredations, from any loss of self-esteem by an admission that the Indians might be humanly their equals. To protect white America from the realization that the Indian was not an inferior being. In order to guarantee that the Indian conformed to the white man's idea of him, the Indian was more and more deprived of his original holdings, since for the white man identity is coextensive with the capacity to own property, to have holdings, and to make a lot of money."

In one word, the ultimate violence which the American white man, like the European white man, has exerted in all unconscious "good faith" upon the colored races of the earth (and above all on the Negro) has been to impose on them *invented identities,* to place them in positions of subservience and helplessness in which they themselves came to believe only in the identities which had thus been conferred upon them.

The ultimate surrender of the Indian is to believe himself a being who belongs on a reservation or in an Indian ghetto, and to remain there without identity, with the possible but generally unreal option of dreaming that he *might* find a place in white society. In the same way the ultimate defeat of the Negro is for him to believe that he is a being who belongs in Harlem, occasionally dreaming that if only he could make it to Park Avenue he would at last become real.

When Radio Station KSSN congratulates the Indians for their war dance, it is congratulating them for accepting an identity imagined for them by somebody else and performing a meaningless, perhaps slightly nostalgic act which defines them as non-persons. The war dance is permitted as an admission of failure. One admits failure by admitting that one is an Indian. A situation worthy of Kafka. To be an Indian is a lifelong desultory exercise in acting as somebody else's invention. But the human incapacity to measure up to such demands constitutes a problem: "the Indian problem." After all, the war dance does remain ambivalent: an assertion that to be an Indian formerly meant something: a capacity for self-defense.

Just as the innocent sounding songs of Negro slaves possessed a deeper meaning, so much dancing too can have a deeper meaning. Dorn's text reminds us of the Massacre of Wounded Knee, December 29th, 1890. Men, women and children were ruthlessly cut down in punishment for the "Ghost Dance," a manifestation of a forbidden and disquieting new Indian con-

sciousness. The Ghost Dance was a desperate appeal to supernatural powers to send a religious Liberator. White America
was having none of that. But Ed Dorn remarks that if the
massacre marked the end of the Ghost Dance, "It also regis-
tered another small installment in the spiritual death of
America."

The intentional ambiguity of Dorn's text is basic and
fruitful, for it shows him to be conscious of the guilt of white
America and totally unsure of the validity of his own pilgrimage of reparation. The photographs of Leroy Lucas are more
direct, more stark, and more accusing. One sees in them the
grinding effect of poverty, suffering, and the mockery of the
pseudo-identity conferred on Indians by the hats, the cars, the
sunglasses, the food, the clothing, the juke boxes of white
America. And one sees the marvelous untouched beauty of
the Indian children, affirming a yet uncontradicted reality
and identity. (But they will learn!)

The most eloquent, moving and hopeful statements in the
book come from one or two Indians who are too articulate
to be white politicians and sociologists. One, for example, a
"literate Indian in Pocatello," argued against Peyotism while
Dorn suggested arguments in its favor. Was the drug not after
all a useful protection against alienation in an impossible
society? Was not the spread of many other drugs an indica-
tion of this? "He allowed that, but on behalf of his own people
he pointed out that they were not natively Western and had,
until white contact, a cosmological sense of a different order,
and while drug taking might be a useful desperateness on the
part of a troubled person in white society, it was at least
possible for an Indian to regain his oneness, because the history of the split was quite short and probably not yet complete
and was perhaps actuated by mere suppression in all its forms,
true, but was not an internalized psychological shifting of
spiritual power as was the case in Western civilization. He
said it is very important for his people to work for their cosmic
identities within the unaltered material of their being, without

the agency of an hallucinogen . . . His point . . . was that a man has as much potential as a plant and should grow by virtue of his own roots."*

Two remarks: first, in spite of the widespread myth that Indians have everywhere used drugs religiously since time immemorial, it must be noted that peyote came to the Shoshoneans only fifty years ago (around 1916). Second, the Indian is still conscious, or able to be conscious, that he is close enough to his own roots to return to them in spite of the violence exercised upon his spirit by the white man. And of course, in so far as a man returns to his own roots, he becomes able to resist exterior violence with complete success and even, after a certain point, invulnerably.

The last four pages of the book are devoted to an admirable statement by a Ponca Indian, Clyde Warrior, originally drafted as a speech for a conference on the War on Poverty. Perhaps the best way to conclude this article would be to quote extensively from the speech. Its wisdom effectively balances the unwisdom of our opening quotation, and makes us feel that America would be better off if we had a few more articulate Indians.

My name is Clyde Warrior and I'm a full blood Ponca Indian from Oklahoma. I appear here before you to try, as much as I can, to present to you the views of Indian youth. If I start my presentation with a slightly cynical quote it is because American Indians generally and Indian youth particu-

---

*The question of peyotism is a very technical and complex one. The peyote cult grew up as a desperate spiritual reaction against the policies of genocide and cultural destruction which were directed against the Plains Indians after the Civil War. Peyote was not merely an escape: it was (and is) considered by the Indian as a way of recovering his identity and spiritual roots in a ground of messianic and apocalyptic vision. However, as the speaker here suggests, there is an essential difference between the cultic use of peyote by the Indians and the use made of it in an entirely different context by whites, though for the same kind of purpose. Indian peyotism cannot simply be dismissed (as it so often has been) as a cultural aberration.

larly are more than a little cynical about programs devised for our betterment. Over the years the federal government has devised programs and "wheeled them" into Indian communities in the name of economic rehabilitation or the like. These programs have, by and large, resulted in bitter divisions and strife in our communities, further impoverishment and the placing of our parents in a more and more powerless position.

I am a young man, but I'm old enough to have seen this process accelerate in my lifetime. This has been the experience of Indian youth—to see our leaders become impotent and less experienced in handling the modern world. Those among our generation who have an understanding of modern life have had to come to that understanding by experiences outside our home communities. The indignity of Indian life, and I would presume the indignity of life among the poor generally in these United States, is the powerlessness of those who are "out of it," but who yet are coerced and manipulated by the very system which excludes them . . .

When I talk to Peace Corps volunteers who have returned from overseas, they tell me, along with many modern historians and economists, that the very structure of the relation between the rich and poor keeps the poor poor; that the powerful do not want change and that it is the very system itself that causes poverty; and that it is just futile to work within this framework. I am not an economist and I cannot evaluate these ideas. I hope that men of good will even among the powerful are willing to have their "boat rocked" a little in order to accomplish the task our country has set itself . . .

As I say I am not sure of the causes of poverty, but one of its correlates at least is this powerlessness, lack of experience, and lack of articulateness . . .

Now we have a new crusade in America—our "War on Poverty"—which purports to begin with a revolutionary new concept—working with the local community. Indian youth could not be more pleased with these kinds of statements, and we hope that for the first time since we were disposed of as a military threat our parents will have something to say about their own destiny and not be ignored as is usually the case. If I am once again a little cynical let me outline the reasons for our fears. I do not doubt that all of you are men of good will and that you do intend to work with the local community. My only fear is what you think the local community is . . .

I do not know how to solve the problem of poverty and I'm not even sure that poverty is what we must solve—perhaps it is only a symptom. In a rich country, like the United States, if poverty is the lack of money and resources that seems to me to be a very small problem indeed. So I cannot say whether poverty is a symptom or a cause or how one would go about solving it in pure economic terms. But of this I am certain, when a people are powerless and their destiny is controlled by the powerful, whether they be rich or poor, they live in ignorance and frustration because they have been deprived of experience and responsibility as individuals and as communities. In the modern world there is no substitute for this kind of experience. One must have it to make rational choices, to live in a world you feel competent to deal with and not be frustrated by. No one can gain this experience without the power to make these decisions himself with his fellows in his local community. No amount of formal education or money can take the place of these basic life experiences for the human being. If the Indian does not understand the modern economy it is because he has never been involved in it. Someone has made those decisions for him. "Handouts" do not erode character. The lack of power over one's own destiny erodes character. And I might add, self-esteem is an important part of character. No one can have competence unless he has both the experience to become competent and make decisions which display competence.

In the old days the Ponca people lived on the buffalo and we went out and hunted it. We believe that God gave the buffalo as a gift to us. That alone did not erode our character, but no one went out and found the buffalo for us and no one organized our hunts for us, nor told how to divide our meats, nor told us how to direct our prayers. We did that ourselves. And we felt ourselves to be a competent, worthy people. In those days we were not "out of the system." We were the system, and we dealt competently with our environment because we had the power to do so. White business men and bureau-

crats did not make the Ponca decisions, the Poncas made those decisions and carried them out. If we were rich one year, it was our doing and if we were poor the next, we felt competent to deal with that condition. Democracy is just not good in the abstract, it is necessary for the human condition; and the epitome of democracy is responsibility as individuals and as communities of people. There cannot be responsibility unless people can make decisions and stand by them or fall by them . . .

I might also add it is only when a community has real freedom that outside help will be effective. The lessons of new nations have certainly taught us that. It was only when colonies in Africa and Asia had their freedom that economic help from France and England became productive. We can apply that lesson here in America to the local community itself.

The speech was never given. This was not permitted. The ideas came too close to the nerve.

WAR AND VISION

THE PRACTICE OF "fasting for vision" was once almost universal among North American Indians for whom it might almost be said that a certain level of "mysticism" was an essential part of growing up. The term mysticism is here used broadly. The Indian based his life on a spiritual illumination beyond the ordinary conscious level of psychic experience. This illumination could probably not be called "supernatural" in a theological sense. (The possibility of supernatural charisma is of course not excluded.) I am not here concerned with the religious content or value of the visions in themselves, but with the fact that such visions were taken for granted as a normal part of life in an archaic culture. They were an essential component in the concept of the mature human personality and hence they were to some extent institutionalized. For although the practice of fasting for vision was an entirely individual project, there was a prescribed ritual and the value of the vision was not decided on the individual's own judgement. The practical consequences of the vision, for good or for evil, could be quite momentous for the rest of the tribe. Hence the chiefs and elders passed judgement on the vision and its interpretation.

It can be said that the vision received after an initiatory period of fasting and solitude was decisive in giving the young Indian a place in the life of his warring and hunting tribe. An Indian without vision could hardly hope to be a great hunter and had no future in the military hierarchy of his people. But of course this was not determined entirely by one initiatory fast. Fasts and solitary retreats were multiplied throughout life and other "psychedelic" expedients were resorted to: ecstatic dancing, self torture, and drugs, which are now well-known, all might be called upon to stimulate the "vision"

17

without which a well-integrated and purposeful existence could hardly be conceived. However, we must not generalize: the use of drugs was far less widespread than dances and fasts for vision.

The nature and content of the vision were not left entirely to chance. It was not just a matter of removing the block of everyday automatisms and the flowering of deeper psychic awareness, though of course in the drug experiences the chemical properties of the drug, producing intense color sensations and so forth, worked in the normal way.

The Indian who fasted for vision sought a personal encounter with a clearly recognizable spirit-friend, a protector whom he felt himself destined to meet, one to whom he felt himself providentially entrusted. This protector was not just any spirit. It was his spirit, his "vision person." And the encounter was not just a matter of seeing and knowing. It was not just "an experience." It changed the course of the seer's entire life: or rather it was what gave his life a "course" to begin with. The meeting, in vision, with "his spirit" set the young Indian upon his life's way. This was the true beginning of his destiny, because henceforth he would be protected, taught, guided, inspired by his vision person. However, guidance was not automatic. Protection and other forms of help could be completely withdrawn if the Indian was not careful, if he disobeyed, and if he was not extremely attentive to every hint or suggestion from his vision person. Such indications were given in dreams, or in the sudden, unexpected appearance of some animal who was the vision person's friend, or in some other event that somehow signalized the presence and concern of the vision person. Finally, of course, one could fast again, or hold a sun dance, for a renewal and clarification of the vision, a deeper encounter, a more intimate familiarity with one's vision person.

The Indian lived in life-long personal companionship with his guardian spirit, encountered usually in the first fast and vision which occurred at the entrance into manhood. He depended immediately and directly on the vision person, especially in his two chief occupations: hunting and war. The vision person gave signs when and where to hunt, where the bison were grazing, and above all he furnished crucially important clues to war strategy: when to plan a raid, when to go on the warpath and when not to. However, the Indian was not left to deal with his vision person alone: the visions and indications required comment and approval from the more experienced men of the tribe, the elders, the medicine men and the chiefs. These were men of authority whose vision persons were very powerful and very friendly. Hence these Indians had a familiar and intimate knowledge of the whole world of the spirits. Indeed they could be assumed to have some acquaintance with the vision persons of others. At least they understood how the spirits usually functioned. In other words, they had a better and more accurate knowledge of the language of vision. The young Indian might interpret his vision in one way, and the elders might proceed to show him that he was quite wrong. He remained free to disobey them and follow his own interpretation, but if he did he ran the risk of disaster. Obedience to his own vision person implied a healthy respect for the opinion of those who understood the spirits, and the elders were most severe in censuring young warriors who "disobeyed their vision person," misguided by passion, temper, ambition or impetuosity. Superstition and vain observance could also antagonize the vision person. One should not be too importunate, too fretful, or multiply too many ritual invocations. There was a right measure to be recognized in everything.

Communion with the vision person was ritually formalized through the use of a "medicine bundle," a little package of magic objects which had been assembled under the explicit direction of the vision person. The ingredients of the medicine bundle were usually fragments of animal skin, bone, rock or herbs: but all these objects were associated in some way or other with the vision person. They were things which he had used to demonstrate his friendly power and were normally revealed in a vision or dream. One prepared for battle or for the hunt with a ceremonious veneration of the vision person, by ritual prayers to the medicine bundle and perhaps also a little impromptu magic suitable to the occasion.

As may easily be guessed, the formalization of relations with the spirits through cult objects easily took the place of vision. Once a culture had passed its peak-vitality, one might expect the medicine bundle to become, in practice, more important than direct communion with the vision person. Then the medicine man became a kind of pharmacist of good luck charms rather than a discerner of spirits.

There is a certain fascination even in dry anthropological studies of Indian culture but there also exist living records of personal experience: the stories told by men who had fasted for vision and who had tried to follow the instructions of their vision person. When we read these stories, we realize that there was really a deep psychological validity to this way of life. It was by no means a mere concoction of superstitious fantasies and mythic explanations of realities that only science could eventually clarify. However one may choose to explain the fact, these stone age people had inherited an archaic wisdom which did somehow protect them against the dangers of a merely superficial, wilful and cerebral existence. It did somehow integrate their personality in such a way that the conscious mind was responsive to deep unconscious sources of awareness. Those who were most in contact with a powerful vision person tended to have an almost phenomenal luck and dexterity in war or in the hunt.

However, we must not be too romantic about all this. There would be no point in merely idealizing primitive men and archaic culture. There is no such thing as a charismatic culture. Though the life of an Indian was much more individualistic than we have imagined, it was integrated in the culture of his tribe and in its complex rituals. "Vision" was perhaps more often a deepening of the common imagination than a real breakthrough of personal insight. Hence there is special interest in the biography of a Crow Indian visionary who, within the framework of this primitive culture and entirely devoted to its values, was a relative failure. Such a story was left by one of the last Crow warriors, Two Leggings, who died at an advanced age in 1923. The record of his conversations, taken down with an interpreter fifty years ago, has now been edited and set (as far as possible) in its accurate historic context, by Peter Nabokov. The book is one of the most fascinating autobiographies published in this century.*

What strikes us immediately is the concept Two Leggings has of biography. What is man's life? It consists primarily in a series of visions. His life is his "medicine." Hs autobiography is in some sense a description of the way his medicine bundle was put together over the years. And the medicine bundle is a kind of concretization of his spiritual and warlike "career." For the most curious thing about Two Leggings is that he is by no means a pure mystic. He is also a career man, and apparently his misfortune was that—in our terms—he tried to make his mysticism serve his career. What we have here then is the life story of a shrewd and intrepid person trying to make his way to the top by a mystique and a magic of success. If we abstract from fasting, vision, and sun-dancing, we can easily translate the formula into a more modern and urban setting.

Within the framework of his cultural establishment, there was nothing unusual about a religious mystique of success. Two Leggings was a very ambitious young Indian, and he was determined to become a chief with the minimum of delay. He was tough, courageous, ruthless, single minded. He was not afraid of fasting or of intense hardship. He could go through the sun dance with all the prescribed tortures, the tearing of the flesh and everything. He followed all the approved formulas for fasting and vision. He sought out dangerous, almost inaccessible places. He fasted on the tops of cliffs. He refused to become tired, discouraged or scared. Even after companions had given up and gone home, he would keep on fasting until he saw *something*. It might not be the top premium vision but at least it was something. When he finally established contact

---

Two Leggings: The Making of a Crow Warrior, by Peter Nabokov. (Thomas Y. Crowell, New York, 1967)

with a reasonably plausible vision person, and began to assemble his bundle, he had highly optimistic ideas of how high the vision person wanted him to go—and how fast. As a result he had some very narrow escapes from death and was not always able to come back to camp in a blaze of glory.

Two Leggings was not beyond faking some spirit-information and on one occasion he even got together a spurious bundle. That time he landed half dead in a creek where he was thrown by an angry bison. In the end, to make sure of having a really good medicine bundle, he purchased one from one of the elders who had the genuine goods. Unfortunately, Two Leggings never realized his ambition of becoming a chief He never got beyond the rank of pipe-holder.

It is an unusually interesting book. The stories of the fasts, the visions, and the subsequent raids, the big bison hunts, the horse stealing forays and the missions of revenge are vividly told. But what is more important is that the psychological reality of the record comes through without static. Two Leggings was not sophisticated enough to be dishonest about his motives. He tells them as they were, frankly admitting that his ambition and impetuosity made him break the rules. He describes himself, perhaps naively, as a determined operator, working with the materials provided by his religious and cultural establishment. He was a man who wanted to count in his society. In order to be someone he had to meet his vision person. He had to convince his vision person he meant business and then the person would let him in on the secret of a really powerful medicine. Having made himself a thoroughly reliable bundle he would get a lot of bison and a lot of scalps. Then he would be a chief and everyone would admit that his medicine was truly potent stuff. He would be a medicine man, and perhaps condescend to share out some of the proven exclusive ingredients with younger men on the way up . . . .

Two Leggings got a lot of scalps and a lot of bison, that was about all. When other Indians of his time heard that his story was being taken down to be put in a book, they said "Why him?" It is true, of course, that one of his visions informed him he would become known all over the earth . . . .

There is something pathetic about the life of Two Leggings,
It would be less pathetic, perhaps, if the visionary element
were mere fantasy. But there was something spiritually and
psychically authentic about the religious culture of the Indians. It helped them to adapt very well indeed to their stone
age situation. Not only that, we must certainly recognize a
universal psychic validity to the concept of encounter with a
"vision person" (purely subjective if you like) as a protector
and mentor in one's chosen way. After all, Catholics still believe (at least some of them) in Guardian Angels. There is
also a universal pathos in the way a spiritual experience, once
ritualized, formalized and fitted into a static establishment,
tends to be manipulated by the ambitions of the believer. It
then becomes self defeating. Vision, systematized and organized
for the sake of personal or institutional aims, becomes blindness. And we all know the story of another kind of vision-
person—one who was on good terms with Faust.

It may be true that Two Legging's medicine continued to
work right up to the end. Perhaps he was right in thinking
that the sight of a white blanket falling out of the sky led him
to the place where he got his last scalp. But then there were
so many other things the vision person did not tell him about.
Two Leggings did not draw any conclusions from the fact that
he followed his enemy along a brand new railway line, or that
in the interval between the shooting and the scalping, he and
his companions spent the rainy night in a section-house with
some white railroad workers.

Up to the end the Crow Indians were so absorbed in their
traditional view of things, their hereditary enmity with the
Piegans and Sioux, that they joined the whites in order to
fight the Sioux. For Two Leggings, this was merely incidental:
it fitted in with his quantitative programme of scalps and
bison. His vision person did not tell him anything about white
men—probably because he himself was not interested. Elsewhere the Indians were seeing new things in visions. They
were being told to drop their fighting among themselves, try

to discover a new, pan-Indian identity, and protect themselves, if they could, against complete extinction. Already the
bison were beginning to disappear. Already the Indians were
being herded into reservations.

Two Leggings' vision person was silent about all this. Two
Leggings did not inquire. The last lines of the book are sad
and heavy with a meaning which this failed chief did not
really see. He knew by now that raiding was forbidden, and
that the white men might punish him for scalping that last
enemy right by their railroad track. In fact he was summoned
to Fort Custer, for an interview with the Commanding Of-
ficer.

> I expected him to put me in prison, but I still went. When I
> entered his room he stood up to shake my hand and I felt better.
> He asked what had happened and after I had finished he said
> that enemies had stolen my horses and I had got them back,
> killing one of the thieves. He said I had done well. When he
> asked if I wanted something to eat I said yes and he went to a
> bureau and took out a coin. Saying he was my friend he told me
> to get something I liked. Again he shook my hand and I thanked
> him. When I got outside I looked at the strange gift. But when
> I went to the store and found all the things I could buy with the
> five dollar gold piece, I understood.

This was a new kind of medicine, and it was associated
with a new kind of war: indeed with a whole new kind of
world, and with a different notion or vision, of life, and of
what made a human being important. In this new world there
was no longer any place for an obsolete bison hunter and stone
age warrior, nor was there any point in fasting for vision. In a
very real sense he was deprived of his full identity. Contact
with his spirit world was broken, because for him this contact
depended entirely on a certain cultural context in which
spirit-guidance gave meaning to his personal ambition. Two
Leggings concludes his story—covering over thirty years in
two and a half lines:

> Nothing happened after that. We just lived. There were no more
> war parties, no capturing of horses from the Piegans and Sioux,
> no buffalo to hunt. There is nothing more to tell.

ISHI: A MEDITATION

G ENOCIDE IS A NEW WORD. Perhaps the word is new because technology has now got into the game of destroying
whole races at once. The destruction of races is not new—
just easier. Nor is it a specialty of totalitarian regimes. We
have forgotten that a century ago white America was engaged
in the destruction of entire tribes and ethnic groups of Indians.
The trauma of California gold. And the vigilantes who, in
spite of every plea from Washington for restraint and understanding, repeatedly took matters into their own hands and
went out slaughtering Indians. Indiscriminate destruction of
the "good" along with the "bad"—just so long as they were
Indians. Parties of riffraff from the mining camps and saloons
suddenly constituted themselves defenders of civilization. They
armed and went out to spill blood and gather scalps. They not
only combed the woods and canyons—they even went into the
barns and ranch houses, to find and destroy the Indian servants and hired people, in spite of the protests of the ranchers
who employed them.

The Yana Indians (including the Yahi or Mill Creeks)
lived around the foothills of Mount Lassen, east of the Sacra-
mento River. Their country came within a few miles of Vina
where the Trappist monastery in California stands today.
These hill tribes were less easy to subdue than their valley
neighbors. More courageous and more aloof, they tried to
keep clear of the white man altogether. They were not necessarily more ferocious than other Indians, but because they kept
to themselves and had a legendary reputation as "fighters,"
they were more feared. They were understood to be completely "savage." As they were driven further and further back
into the hills, and as their traditional hunting grounds gradually narrowed and emptied of game, they had to raid the
ranches in order to keep alive. White reprisals were to be expected, and they were ruthless. The Indians defended them-

selves by guerilla warfare. The whites decided that there could be no peaceful coexistence with such neighbors. The Yahi, or Mill Creek Indians, as they were called, were marked for complete destruction. Hence they were regarded as sub-human. Against them there were no restrictions and no rules. No treaties need be made for no Indian could be trusted. Where was the point in "negotiation?"

Ishi, the last survivor of the Mill Creek Indians, whose story was published by the University of California at Berkeley in 1964*, was born during the war of extermination against his people. The fact that the last Mill Creeks were able to go into hiding and to survive for another fifty years in their woods and canyons is extraordinary enough. But the courage, the resourcefulness, and the sheer nobility of these few stone age men struggling to preserve their life, their autonomy and their identity as a people rises to the level of tragic myth. Yet there is nothing mythical about it. The story is told with im-peccable objectivity—though also with compassion—by the scholars who finally saved Ishi and learned from him his language, his culture, and his tribal history.

To read this story thoughtfully, to open one's heart to it, is to receive a most significant message: one that not only moves, but disturbs. You begin to feel the inner stirrings of that pity and dread which Aristotle said were the purifying effect of tragedy. "The history of Ishi and his people," says the author, Theodora Kroeber, "is inexorably part of our own history. We have absorbed their lands into our holdings. Just so must we be the responsible custodians of their tragedy, absorbing it into our tradition and morality." Unfortunately, we learned little or nothing about ourselves from the Indian wars.

"They have separated murder into two parts and fastened the worse on me"—words which William Carlos Williams put on the lips of a Viking Exile, Eric the Red. Men are always

*Ishi In Two Worlds: A biography of the last wild Indian in North America, by Theodora Kroeber. (University of California Press, Berkeley, 1964).

separating murder into two parts: one which is unholy and unclean: for "the enemy." Another which is a sacred duty: "for our side." He who first makes the separation, in order that he may kill, proves his bad faith. So too in the Indian wars. Why do we always assume the Indian was the aggressor? We were in *his* country, we were taking it over for ourselves, and we likewise refused even to share any with him. We were the people of God, always in the right, following a manifest destiny. The Indian could only be a devil. But once we allow ourselves to see all sides of the question, the familiar perspectives of American history undergo a change. The "savages" suddenly become human and the "whites," the "civilized," can seem barbarians. True, the Indians were often cruel and inhuman (some more than others). True also, the humanity, the intelligence, the compassion and understanding which Ishi met with in his friends the scholars, when he came to join our civilization, restore the balance in our favor. But we are left with a deep sense of guilt and shame. The record is there. The Mill Creek Indians, who were once seen as bloodthirsty devils, were peaceful, innocent and deeply wronged human beings. In their use of violence they were, so it seems, generally very fair. It is we who were the wanton murderers, and they who were the innocent victims. The loving kindness lavished on Ishi in the end did nothing to change that fact. His race had been barbarously, pointlessly destroyed.

The impact of the story is all the greater because the events are so deeply charged with a natural symbolism: the structure of these happenings is such that it leaves a haunting imprint on the mind. Out of that imprint come disturbing and potent reflections.

Take for example the scene in 1870 when the Mill Creeks were down to their last twenty or thirty survivors. A group had been captured. A delegation from the tiny remnant of the tribe appeared at a ranch to negotiate. In a symbolic gesture, they handed over five bows (five being a sacred number) and stood waiting for an answer. The gesture was not properly understood, though it was evident that the Indians were trying to recover their captives and promising to abandon all hostilities. In effect, the message was: "Leave us alone, in peace, in our hills, and we will not bother you any more. We are few, you are many, why destroy us? We are no longer any menace to you." No formal answer was given. While the Indians were waiting for some intelligible response, one of the whites slung a rope over the branch of a tree. The Indians quietly withdrew into the woods.

From then on, for the next twelve years, the Yahi disappeared into the hills without a trace. There were perhaps twenty of them left, one of whom was Ishi, together with his mother and sister. In order to preserve their identity as a tribe, they had decided that there was no alternative but to keep completely away from white men, and have nothing whatever to do with them. Since co-existence was impossible, they would try to be as if they did not exist for the white man at all. To be there as if they were not there.

In fact, not a Yahi was seen. No campfire smoke rose over the trees. Not a trace of fire was found. No village was discovered. No track of an Indian was observed. The Yahi remnant (and that phrase takes on haunting biblical resonances) systematically learned to live as invisible and as unknown.

To anyone who has ever felt in himself the stirrings of a monastic or solitary vocation, the notion is stirring. It has implications that are simply beyond speech. There is nothing one can say in the presence of such a happening and of its connotations for what our spiritual books so glibly call "the hidden life." The "hidden life" is surely not irrelevant to our modern world; nor is it a life of spiritual comfort and tranquillity which a chosen minority can happily enjoy, at the price of a funny costume and a few prayers. The "hidden life" is the extremely difficult life that is forced upon a remnant that has to stay completely out of sight in order to escape destruction.

This so called "long concealment" of the Mill Creek Indians is not romanticized by any means. The account is sober, objective, though it cannot help being an admiring tribute to the extraordinary courage and ingenuity of these lost stone-age people. Let the book speak for itself.

> The long concealment failed in its objective to save a people's life but it would seem to have been brilliantly successful in its psychology and techniques of living . . . . Ishi's group was a master of the difficult art of communal and peaceful coexistence in the presence of alarm and in a tragic and deteriorating prospect . . . .
> It is a curious circumstance that some of the questions which arise about the concealment are those for which in a different context psychologists and neurologists are trying to find answers for the submarine and outer space services today. Some of these are: what makes for morale under confining and limiting life-conditions? What are the presumable limits of claustrophobic endurance? . . . It seems that the Yahi might have qualified for outer space had they lasted into this century.

There is something challenging and awe inspiring about this thoughtful passage by a scientifically trained mind. And that phrase about "qualifying for outer space" has an eerie ring about it. Does someone pick up the half-heard suggestion that the man who wants to live a normal life span during the next two hundred years of our history must be the kind of person who is "qualified for outer space?" Let us return to Ishi. The following sentences are significant:

> In contrast to the Forty niners . . . . whose morality and morale had crumbled, Ishi and his band remained incorrupt, humane, compassionate, and with their faith intact even unto starvation, pain and death. The questions then are: what makes for stability? For psychic strength? For endurance, courage, faith?

The answers given by the author to these questions are mere suggestions. The Yahi were on their own home ground. This idea is not developed. The reader should reflect a little on the relation of the Indian to the land on which he lived. In this sense, most modern men never know what it means to have a "home ground." Then there is a casual reference to the "American Indian mystique" which could also be developed. William Faulkner's hunting stories, particularly "The Bear," give us some idea of what this "mystique" might involve. The word "mystique" has unfortunate connotations: it suggests an

emotional icing on an ideological cake. Actually the Indian
lived by a deeply religious wisdom which can be called in a
broad sense mystical, and that is certainly much more than "a
mystique." The book does not go into religious questions very
deeply, but it shows us Ishi as a man sustained by a deep and
unassailable spiritual strength which he never discussed.

Later, when he was living "in civilization" and was something of a celebrity as well as an object of charitable concern,
Ishi was questioned about religion by a well-meaning lady.
Ishi's English was liable to be unpredictable, and the language
of his reply was not within its own ironic depths of absurdity:

"Do you believe in God?" the lady inquired.
"Sure, Mike!" he retorted briskly.

There is something dreadfully eloquent about this innocent
short-circuit in communication.

One other very important remark is made by the author.
The Yahi found strength in the incontrovertible fact that they
were in the right. *"Of very great importance to their psychic
health was the circumstance that their suffering and curtail-
ments arose from wrongs done to them by others.* They were
not guilt ridden."

Contrast this with the spectacle of our own country with
its incomparable technological power, its unequalled material
strength, and its psychic turmoil, its moral confusion and its
profound heritage of guilt which neither the righteous declara-
tions of Cardinals nor the moral indifference of "realists" can
do anything to change! Every bomb we drop on a defenseless
Asian village, every Asian child we disfigure or destroy with
fire, only adds to the moral strength of those we wish to destroy for our own profit. It does not make the Viet Cong
cause just; but by an accumulation of injustice done against
innocent people we drive them into the arms of our enemies
and make our own ideals look like the most pitiful sham.

Gradually the last members of the Yahi tribe died out.
The situation of the survivors became more and more desperate. They could not continue to keep up their perfect in-
visibility: they had to steal food. Finally the hidden camp

where Ishi lived with his sister and sick mother was discovered by surveyors who callously walked off with the few objects they found as souvenirs. The mother and sister died and finally on August 29, 1911, Ishi surrendered to the white race, expecting to be destroyed.

Actually, the news of this "last wild Indian" reached the anthropology department at Berkeley and a professor quickly took charge of things. He came and got the "wild man" out of jail. Ishi spent the rest of his life in San Francisco, patiently teaching his hitherto completely unknown (and quite sophisticated) language to experts like Sapir. Curiously enough, Ishi lived in an anthropological museum where he earned his living as a kind of caretaker and also functioned, on occasion, as a live exhibit. He was well treated, and in fact the affection and charm of his relations with his white friends are not the least moving part of his story. He adapted to life in the city without too much trouble and returned once, with his friends, to live several months in his old territory, under his natural conditions, showing them how the Yahi had carried out the fantastic operation of their invisible survival. But he finally succumbed to one of the diseases of civilization. He died of tuberculosis in 1916, after four and a half years among white men.

For the reflective reader who is—as everyone must be to-day—deeply concerned about man and his fate, this is a moving and significant book, one of those unusually suggestive works that *must* be read, and perhaps more than once. It is a book to think deeply about and to take notes on, not only because of its extraordinary factual interest but because of its special quality as a kind of parable.

One cannot help thinking today of the Viet Nam war in terms of the Indian wars of a hundred years ago. Here again, one meets the same myths and misunderstandings, the same obsession with "completely wiping out" an enemy regarded as diabolical. The language of the Vigilantes had overtones of puritanism in it. The backwoods had to be "completely cleaned out," or "purified" of Indians—as if they were vermin. I have read accounts of American GI's taking the same attitude toward the Viet Cong. The jungles are thought to be "infested" with communists, and hence one goes after them as one would go after ants in the kitchen back home. And in this process of "cleaning up" (the language of "cleansing" appeases and pacifies the conscience,) one becomes without realizing it a murderer of women and children. But this is an unfortunate accident, what the moralists call "double effect." Something that is just too bad, but which must be accepted in view of something more important that has to be done. And so there is more and more killing of civilians and less and less of the "something more important" which is what we are trying to achieve. In the end, it is the civilians that are killed in the ordinary course of events, and combatants only get killed by accident. No one worries any more about double effect. War is waged against the innocent to "break enemy morale."

What is most significant is that Viet Nam seems to have become an extension of our old western frontier, complete with enemies of another "inferior" race. This is a real "new frontier" that enables us to continue the cowboys-and-indians game which seems to be part and parcel of our national identity. What a pity that so many innocent people have to pay with their lives for our obsessive fantasies.

One last thing. Ishi never told anyone his real name. The California Indians apparently never uttered their own names, and were very careful about how they spoke the names of others. Ishi would never refer to the dead by name either. "He never revealed his own private Yahi name," says the author. "It was as though it had been consumed in the funeral pyre of the last of his loved ones."

In the end, no one ever found out a single name of the vanished community. Not even Ishi's. For Ishi simply means MAN.

PART II

THE CROSS FIGHTERS

NOTES ON A RACE WAR

T HE TRAUMATIC CLASH between races is one of the standard problems of our time. Everywhere it tends to take somewhat the same form. The purpose of this essay is not historical, still less political. It is intended as a study of the human and cultural elements in a typical case of interracial conflict. I am particularly interested in the ways in which an oppressed and humiliated "primitive" civilization seeks to recover its identity and to maintain itself in independence, against the overwhelming threat of a society which can rely on unlimited backing from the great powers, precisely because it is white.

1

Yucatán in 1847 was hardly what one would call a "great power." It had fairly recently become independent of Spain and was now undecided about accepting incorporation into Mexico. Yucatán wanted to be an autonomous nation but it could hardly stand on its own feet. It was split by political parties that were always ready to take up arms against each other and which also sought to make use of Indian manpower in their internecine struggles.

The Maya Indians, overcome by Spain three hundred years before, exhausted by war and disease, had been allowed to survive with their traditional *ejido* system. In many parts of Guatemala and Yucatán they were isolated in their own communities. This setup was disrupted by the new government. Indians were forced into debt peonage on the haciendas that began to grow rich on henequen. Independence from Spain and "liberal" government brought no special advantage to the Maya. On the contrary, the new system meant greater instability, it uprooted the Maya from his village communities and his beloved cornfields. It threw him into closer contact with the

Ladino and *mestizo* whom he consequently came to know better and trust even less than before. This close contact between races served only to emphasize the fundamental contrast between two ways of life: that of the Indian, essentially rural, hierarchic and religious, and that of the white in towns, cities or on big haciendas, more and more frankly secular and antireligious (though welcoming the help of the Church in "keeping order").

The conflict between the Mayans and the Ladinos of Yucatán was more properly a cultural and a caste war rather than a battle between two races. It is in fact known in history as the *Guerra de las Castas.* Whereas in the United States the racial character of the conflict between Black and White is brought out by the fact that a Negro with white blood is classified as a Negro whether he likes it or not, in Yucatán an Indian with white blood is a *mestizo* and may, in effect, choose one side or the other. Generally his choice is for the white culture. He tries, as far as possible, to live like a Ladino, and no one hinders his integration in the society. His problem is economic rather than racial.

Speaking of the situation in Yucatán at the time when the Caste War began (1847-1848) the best authority on the subject* says:

> We know the country was divided by race, but even more it was split by opposing conceptions of a common world. Corn, a mere commodity to the white man, was sacred to the Maya; for the white man uncultivated land was simply waste land, but for the Maya it was the rightful home of the forest gods.

Of course it must be remembered that the Maya had accepted Christianity wholeheartedly. The remarkable synthesis of Christian, Biblical ideas with the vestiges of a Mayan social structure, built on the elaborate and quasi-mystical calendar system that went back to the days before Christ, took on a profound eschatological character in the Mayan books of Chilam

---

*Nelson Reed, in *The Caste War of Yucatán,* Stanford University Press Paperback (SP 52) reprint 1967.

Balam. Those prophetic and apocalyptic books had been preserved and studied in secret since the time of the Conquest, and they hinted at the coming retribution that was to be visited upon the conquerors from the rising sun, not because they were Christians but more precisely because they were *not* Christians.

It is curious to see with what fervor some of the Maya prophets at the same time accepted the message of Christ and rejected the messengers as unworthy (while admitting the need for Catholic priests as mediators). In the Chilam Balam book of Chumayel we read the following appraisal of the Conquest:

> The "most Christian" men arrived here with the true God; but that was the beginning of our misery, the beginning of tribute, the beginning of "charity," the cause of secret discord coming to light, the beginning of fighting with guns . . . the beginning of debt slavery and of debts pinned to the shoulders . . .
>
> This was Antichrist on earth, the tiger of peoples, the mountain cat of nations, drinking the blood of the poor Indian. But the day is coming when the tears of the Indians' eyes will reach God and the justice of God will descend upon the world with one crashing blow!

There had been a brief rebellion, brutally suppressed, in the mid-eighteenth century. Now, in the ferment of restless change, the Mayans were beginning to evaluate the new situation in their own terms, which were those of Chilam Balam. We know that the book was once more in circulation (the printed Spanish edition of the Chilam Balam of Chumayel is based on a manuscript that changed hands in 1831) and the Indians were reinterpreting their role in the revolutionary world of the time: they must once more affirm their own identity and repudiate the wicked society of their conquerors, and perhaps even prepare the way for the judgment of God. Indeed, it might turn out that they themselves were instruments of that judgment. Obviously such ideas were mulled over by a few in secret and were not widely published. But they had their effect.

In the eyes of the Maya the "unchristian" character of the Ladino society seemed evident not so much from a lack of formal orthodoxy as from a contempt for man, for growing and living things, for the land, for the sacred corn plant, the gift of the gods - and for the Indian himself. A spokesman for the Mayan Indians summed up the reason why they intended to resist the whites, if necessary, by violence.

> We poor Indians are aware of what the whites are doing to injure us, of how many evils they commit against us, even to our children and harmless women. So much injury without basis seems to us a crime . . . If the Indians revolt, it is because the whites gave them reason; because the whites say they do not believe in Jesus Christ, because they have burned the cornfield. They have given just cause for the reprisals of the Indians, whom they themselves have killed . . .

(The declaration continues that no matter what force the whites use against them, the Mayans are not going to give up because . . .)

> We are God's sacrifices. They will have to say whether God gave them permission to slaughter us all, and that we have no will in the matter . . . Therefore, if we die at the hands of the whites, patience. The whites think that these things are ended, but never. It is so written in the book of Chilam Balam, and even so has said Our Lord Jesus Christ on earth and beyond, that if the whites become peaceful, so shall we become peaceful.
>
> *Quoted in Reed, op. cit., pp. 48-49*

2

Unfortunately the whites could not "become peaceful." The Indian who had spoken these words was apprehended and shot. All the others now saw clearly what they themselves could expect. The lesson was driven home still more clearly when the farm of one of the Maya leaders was sacked and the women raped by whites in July 1847. The leader himself struck back on a white village, massacring the Ladinos and thus bringing on even more furious reprisals: several Indian villages were destroyed with atrocities and the desecration of churches by whites. A change was made in the Constitution, Indians were stripped of their recently gained civil rights, the whipping posts of colonial times were set up again, and peaceful Mayas were apprehended, tortured and made to "confess" an imaginary plot for a general massacre in the capital city of Mérida.

In fact, the white population was now seized by racist hysteria. A draft was proclaimed to raise an army of defence, with the warning "only whites need apply." In a short time seventeen percent of the Ladino population was under arms. (10% of the U. S. population was under arms at the height of World War II.) Meanwhile the women of Mérida, on the night of the imaginary massacre, were waiting with jars of boiling water to pour from the rooftops on the expected rapists and killers.

The war actually began in September 1847. When one of the (white) political leaders of Yucatán tried to seize power, and the army moved to prevent him, the Indians ravaged the area of Valladolid, and acquired enough money from the haciendas to buy guns and ammunition in British Honduras. The fight was on.

In February 1848 the Indians who had risen in force all over eastern Yucatán, were besieging Valladolid and it was evident that the situation was serious.

At this point the Church spoke out for peace and letters were sent to the Indians urging that they desist and withdraw. Bishops took the opportunity to issue the now familiar denunciations of godlessness, secularism, freemasonry and so on, suggesting that the horrors of war had been sent in punishment for all these evils. Unfortunately, as Reed observes, there were no freemasons among the Indians. The Mayan leaders replied to this fervent Christian appeal:

> And now you remember that there is a True God. While you were murdering us didn't you know that there was a True God? You were always recommending the name of God to us and you never believed in His Name . . . . And now you are not prepared nor

have you the courage to accept the exchange for your blows. If
we are killing now, you first showed us the way . . . Twenty four
hours we allow you to give up your arms. If you are prompt,
no harm will come to you nor to your houses, but the houses
and haciendas of all whites who do not give up their arms will
be burned, and they will be killed besides, because that's how
they have taught us; thus everything the whites have done to us,
we shall do the same and more.

Another leader wrote less truculently and in some detail,
pleading with one of the bishops for a genuine settlement of
Indian grievances: protection against arbitrary violence on the
part of whites, relief from an intolerable burden of taxation,
and a lower "price" for Baptism and Marriage as well as for
other religious ceremonies.

The Indians are fighting, he says,

. . . to defend themselves against the killing that the sub-delegate
Antonio Trujeque started among us . . . He began the fires,
burning the town of Tepich and he began to catch the poor Indians as you catch animals in the woods . . . The Indians don't
know if the superior government has given orders that they should
be killed, and they won't stop until the government has made a
pronouncement . . .

Both quotations from Reed, p. 78

Peace talks failed, and in March the whites prepared to
evacuate Valladolid. But when an accident blocked the road,
the column of withdrawing troops and refugees was slaugh-
tered by the Indians, and all Yucatán was thrown into panic.

It was at this point that the government of Yucatán began
sending out desperate appeals for help to the great powers,
even offering Yucatán as a colony to anyone who would come
in and deliver the Ladinos from this menace of destruction. A
bill to aid Yucatán was introduced in the U. S. Congress but
was dropped when, in March, news came of a peace treaty
which had given the Mayans "all that they asked for." Unfortunately this treaty was only a trick with a dual purpose of
stalling for time and dividing the Maya leaders against each
other. It failed, and the Mayan armies advanced with further
victories.

By May of 1848 the Indians were in control of most of Yucatán. Three columns were reaching out for Mérida, the capital, and others were advancing on the eastern port of Campeche. The whites had been pushed all the way to the east coast and many were leaving the country on anything that could float, even though the government had passed a law forbidding emigration. The Bishop of Mérida departed for Havana and the Governor had actually written out a proclamation declaring the evacuation of the capital, but it could not be printed because there was no paper in the city. The Governor packed up and prepared to go south to Campeche, for a last stand against the onslaught that would probably bring victory to the Indians and make them masters of Yucatán. But the final attack never came.

What happened?

The difference between two utterly opposed world views had led to the war, and it was the difference between those two world views that led the Indians to relax their grasp on certain victory. The son of one of the leaders gave the following explanation, years later.

> (When the army was before Mérida) . . . all at once the winged ants, harbingers of the first rain, appeared in great clouds . . . When my father's people saw this they said to themselves and to their brothers "Ehen! The time has come for us to make our planting, for if we do not we shall have no grace of God to fill the bellies of our children . . ."

The next morning, the Mayan soldiers said to their Chiefs "we are going" and with rolled up blankets, started home to their cornfields. Then the Chiefs went into council and decided that there was nothing left but for them to go home too.

The Indian rebellion was in a certain sense a political. The leaders did indeed formulate clear and reasonable political demands, but the thinking of the Mayan masses was not political and even the leaders had no long range objectives. Though they were now capable of taking over the whole Yucatán Peninsula by military force, the Mayans showed by their actions that they were not interested, and that if they had gained power in Yucatán they would not have known what to do with it. In fact, one may surmise that they themselves were as surprised as anybody else at their own extraordinary military success. Their refusal to take advantage of it was an admission that they had reached the limit of what they could cope with, politically, culturally and psychologically. What happened then was a curious regression, a falling back upon psychological positions that were familiar and traditional. These positions were basically peaceful, constructive, humanly healthy. But from the point of view of modern political life this instinctive regression was a disaster, and modern man can only look upon it as a complete collapse of reason, a farcical proof of our contention that primitive races are "inferior." The Mayans failed because they did not know one of the main axioms of modern life, an axiom on which is based the American pragmatic imperative to push for the competitor's unconditional defeat. "In war there is no substitute for complete victory." The Mayans failed because they were still too willing to listen to the voice of peaceful and constructive human instinct—a voice which has to be silenced if efficiency is to be total.

3

The whites immediately regained all that they had lost, pushing the Indians back into the western jungle and, incidentally, harvesting their cornfields in the following summer. With this sudden change of fortune, the whites now had everything on their side, including some Indians of the west coast who had not been properly informed about what was really going on. There were also some volunteers from the U. S., men who had been mustered out at Mobile after the Mexican war and thought Yucatán was going to be fun, just like Texas. They were disillusioned. (Incidentally, much later on, a group of American Confederates who had moved to British Honduras after the Civil War fought Maya raiders there in 1872.) The Ladino forces were now receiving aid from abroad and the

Indians, who had so far subsisted on what they took from towns and haciendas, had practically run out of supplies.

Nevertheless, the war did not end. It merely entered a new stage. The southwest jungle area of what is now called Quintana Roo remained Maya territory and eventually became what was *de facto* a separate Maya nation where whites might hazard raids but not with impunity.

Meanwhile, the population of Yucatán had been *cut in half* in four years of war. The Governor, a Liberal Democrat and former "friend of the Indians," was now raising funds by selling captured Mayas to Cuba as slaves, on ten year work contracts (from which of course they never returned). With the proceeds of these transactions, the Governor financed an expedition against a small fortified town in the southwest in order to have a beachhead in the Maya-controlled area. Later, another such expedition was financed by loans on the anticipated sale of Indian war prisoners to Cuba. When the whites were beaten, friendly Maya were sent to Cuba to pay the debt instead.

What happened now was perhaps the most significant thing in the whole war. Forced back into the jungle—which was after all their natural habitat in any case—cut off from all direct contact with white society except for British Honduras, where they procured their arms, cut off even from the Catholic Church on whose priests and sacraments they had hitherto depended in spiritual things, the Indians now began the creation of a new segregated society of their own. It was not a return to ancient traditional Mayan civilization. The memory of that had been more or less effectively wiped out in three hundred years. It was not Ladino Catholicism. It was not a *mestizo* imitation of white society. It was an authentic, Indian society built of Christian and Indian elements fused together in an organism with a complete and fully coherent identity of its own. In other words, the Indians of the Southwest jungles successfully formed a separatist nation based on an ethos of resistance and on the refusal of white domination.

The religious and apocalyptic character of the society, its military and prophetic identity, made it an exemplar of the structures which many racial resistance groups and nativistic movements have been building in the last hundred years. It reproduces familiar historic patterns - notably that of the Maccabbean resistance in Post-exilic Judaism: the ideal climate for apocalyptic literature.

The resistance of the jungle Maya was built around a religious-military capital, a shrine called Chan Santa Cruz. This was not a city, but a focus of religious activity like the ancient Maya cult centers. The archaic Mayan "city" was in fact a collection of tombs, temples, ceremonial ball-courts, observatories and so on, where the social and religious life of the people came to a focus, where the complex evolutions of the Mayan calendar were worked out, and where men and Gods met in worship and in prophetic guidance. Chan Santa Cruz reproduced this pattern on a much smaller and rudimentary scale, in a Christian instead of an archaic Mayan form. The Indians of the resistance lived, like their forefathers, in small villages scattered through the jungle which they cleared for corn in small slash-and-burn plots (*milpas*). They came together at Chan Santa Cruz for religious worship and for prophetic instruction which was delivered, in times of crisis, by the "miraculous" Speaking Cross enshrined there.

We still do not know nearly enough about the ancient Mayan religion and philosophy of life to judge it correctly. Obviously the decadent religion of pre-Conquest times does not tell the whole story, still less the vestiges of superstition magic, prophecy and so on which continued after the Conquest. Maya religion of the classic period was centered in a complex cosmic and liturgical mystique of time cycles in which the directives of the gods to their people were interpreted by a sophisticated system of mathematics, historic chronicle, art and religious rite. Later, the veneration of votive objects, statues and other things kept in hiding and perhaps endowed with speech, kept people in contact with what the gods, and eventually what Christ and His saints, demanded of them. The books of Chilam Balam were supposed to have been directed by mysterious voices. When the Maya came together it was second nature to them to want to hear God speak, and speak directly: not in the words of a book or of a medium or through a prophet. The key idea in the understanding of the "Speaking Cross" is then the Maya's need for direct contact with the True God, the God of the Bible and of Christ, not through a Church of Ladinos who had proved themselves murderers, cheats and liars. The Maya wanted to hear God speak in their own convocations, and they were convinced that He would do so because they felt they were His people.

Now much has been made of the fact that the "speaking" of this Cross was produced by ventriloquism. Recognizing the psychological importance of the Speaking Cross, the Ladinos made special efforts to discredit it. The war on the Indian became, in a special way, a war on the Speaking Cross. By unmasking the "deceit" of the Cross and destroying the Indian's faith in it, the Ladino hoped to shatter the Indian's sense of community and identity and reduce him to cultural and psychological dependence. And this seemed to him to be almost absurdly easy. All he had to do was show that the Cross did not work miracles, that it was a fanatical, superstitious myth, and so on. Hence repeated attacks and raids were made on Chan Santa Cruz, as long as it remained a defenseless village of huts, where the Cross was displayed on the trunk of a sacred Jungle Tree. The Ladinos concentrated with impassioned intensity on the Cross as material object and on the "voice" as a material fraud, convinced that this was the way to strike the heart of the Indian's resistance. In 1851, the Cross was stolen. It was immediately replaced by another. In 1852 the supposedly miraculous tree was cut down and later on the ventriloquist arrangement (a pit in which the speaker was hidden) was exposed and ridiculed. None of this had any effect on the Indians who remained passionately devoted to the Cross and believed everything it said to them.

Was this an "intentional deception?" Or was it a kind of prophetic rite? The workings of the system were known to the Indians themselves. They were aware that a man was speaking, yet they still elected to believe that God was speaking to them through him and that the words, whatever their immediate source, were prophetic. They were the "Words of the Cross" uttered in their sacred assembly.

4

The phenomenon of Chan Santa Cruz, in this as in other respects, resembles the Cargo cults which sprang up later in Melanesia, Polynesia and elsewhere. There too, confusion, frustration, resistance, and a desperate attempt to cope with the economic, social and spiritual disruption colonialism had produced in native society, led to spontaneous emergence of apocalyptic and nativistic groups. Men obeyed voices, centered seemingly absurd hopes on promises of prophets. Mysterious cult objects appeared—or imitation radio-stations and air-strips invited communication with an affluent world of an-cestors. In the Cargo cults also we find an intense *will to be-lieve* in prophetic promises which are often, from our view-point, wildly irrational and utterly hopeless. In the Cargo cults there is in fact a far greater residue of magic thinking mixed up with a semi-Christian eschatology than we find at Chan Santa Cruz.

In either case, however, the religious phenomenon is ab-solutely central to the resistance and the militancy of the movement. Hence, rather than trying to "explain" the ap-parent irrationality or fanaticism of the movement by tracing it to an obvious hoax, we would do better to consider the phenomenon—in this case the Speaking Cross—as a spon-taneous living expression of the new sense of community and identity which has been called into being by a spirit of re-sistance. In other words, instead of spelling it out in our cause-and-effect terms by saying: "religious fakers persuade the people that they have been commanded by God to resist the whites," we should understand it in some such terms as these: "the overwhelming need to recover a sense of community and identity, in order to resist the whites successfully, made the Indians singly and collectively devote an intense energy of faith to the worship which was the heart of their resistance movement."

Just as Camus's newspaper, *Combat,* was an articulate voice of the French resistance, denying and challenging all the claims made by the Nazis in occupied France, so the Speaking Cross was, for a more primitive and religious-minded people, the articulate voice of their own resistance, guaranteeing their identity, affirming their right to resist, and giving them the strength to do so. The words of a quavering voice in the dark were not by themselves sufficient to do this; but the spirit of community and the sense of solidarity which resulted from their common will to unite against their enemies required this dramatic expression: the rite and mystery appropriate to a small, embattled, apocalyptic group, convinced that it was the victim of great injustice and believing that the Indians were under the judgment of God for the wrongs done to the Indians.

The importance of this cannot be neglected. In the first place, we must admit that the Indians were quite right: they had been treated with monstrous injustice—and those of them who submitted to white society continued to be so. In the second place, the *Cruzob* or people of the Cross, who gathered together in the resistance movement around Chan Santa Cruz, were the only Mayas who managed to retain a clearcut social identity and dignity of their own, while other Mayans drifted away and more or less disintegrated under white pressure. The *Cruzob* at least maintained a social order of their own. They maintained a culture that was completely independent of the white Ladinos and was fully capable of protecting itself against them. In Reed's words, the *Cruzob* resistance produced "the only creative response of the rebel Maya to the attack on their world view." Under the shock of war and the threat of annihilation, but favored by the protecting jungle in which they could travel light with few needs and could outwit the white man in guerilla war, the Indians not only survived but created "a unique example of Spanish Indian cultural synthesis . . . a real synthesis on more than the village level."

5

The theocratic military society of the *Cruzob* was a radical adaptation of traditional Mayan village life. It involved an instinctive return to many ancient patterns and structures. Communal and democratic to a degree, the society depended on the dedication of its members and on their willingness to perform their various offices, to take their turn at guard duty (which was demanded of every healthy man over sixteen) besides cultivating their own cornfields and participating in the more or less elaborate hierarchical system of worship and celebrating characteristic of Indian society. In spite of obvious distortions, Chan Santa Cruz does give us some hints about life in ancient Maya cities which, in the classic period, must have depended not on slave labor but on the willing cooperation of free men who took pride in the sacred cities which they had built with their own hands and where they enjoyed the splendid religious festivities which filled their lives both with meaning and with pleasure. (It must always be remembered that human sacrifice, slavery and other by-products of war were *not* characteristic of the most ancient classic Maya society: they were brought in by the Toltecs and Aztecs when Mayan culture began to decline.)

In the beginning of the resistance, and during the war, the devout Catholic Maya depended to a great extent on captured priests in order to have Mass, sacraments, and other religious celebrations which they felt to be essential. The *Cruzob* had to make a rather radical decision: to get along without priests, in order to be completely independent of Ladino society. Indians who had good memories and who had learned the Latin prayers as altar boys, or seminarians, officiated not only in singing the Salve Regina and other anthems highly valued by the Indians, but also in "saying Mass" which was offered with tortillas of corn and honey. At Chan Santa Cruz—as also in some European monastic communities at that time—there were two Community Masses each day in the shrine: the first an early Low Mass, the second a late High Mass complete with band music. The *Cruzob* had a taste for this kind of thing, and in 1860 when they drove off a white expedition with a smashing defeat, they took great care to capture all the band alive with their instruments, and set them to teaching the children how to play cornets, trombones and clarinets.

There were, in fact, slaves at Chan Santa Cruz: Ladinos and *mestizos* who had been captured in raids, and also some Chinese. Where did the Chinese come from? In 1866 the S. S. *Light of Ages* landed at Belize, British Honduras, with 480 coolies from Amoy to work in the logging camps. Anyone who has read Traven's *Rebellion of the Hanged* has some idea of what life in the logging camps was like. The coolies shrewdly sized up the situation and one hundred of them took off into Yucatán. Four of these eventually got to Mérida where they opened a laundry, but most of the hundred did not make it through *Cruzob* territory. They were taken as slaves. They probably did better than the others who remained in the camps and rapidly died of fever.

The *Cruzob* subsisted for over fifty years as a *de facto* separate nation (Reed has an amusing account of an interview of an envoy from British Honduras with the Speaking Cross. The Cross took a dislike to the envoy and the interview was unpleasant.) In 1884 the *Cruzob* even came to a formal agreement with Mexico which recognized their right to autonomous existence and guaranteed them against attack, provided they consented to form part, at least theoretically, of the Mexican nation. This treaty was without effect, but the fact that it could be made was significant.

Life in the jungles of Chan Santa Cruz was never paradisaic. Though the war petered out in 1851 due to the disintegration of the Yucatán army (the men were starving and deserted by the hundred), Chan Santa Cruz was constantly threatened. The whites of Northern and Western Yucatán did not want the *Cruzob* even as remote neighbors. Expeditions were frequently sent out against them, and the *Cruzob* in their turn raided white settlements along their borders. But the *Cruzob* population declined. So did the morale. Finally, in 1901, under the dictatorship of Díaz, an army was sent to clean out the *Cruzob* territory and run a railway through it. This job was done by a brutal and unscrupulous General called Inacio Bravo who liked to torture Indians and burn them alive. Bravo made a fortune out of Quintana Roo where he had a hand in everything that went on. He furnished (Mexican) political prisoners to the logging camps at 25 pesos a head F.O.B. Vera Cruz. Chan Santa Cruz became the capital of the new state, and was renamed Santa Cruz de Bravo in honor of the General who had at last brought civilization.

Even then, the story did not end. A revolution got rid of Díaz and put in Madero. A Yucatán revolutionary leader gave Santa Cruz back to the Maya (in 1915). The remaining *Cruzob* who had been hiding in the jungle returned, destroyed the railway and the telegraph, refused to reoccupy the desecrated town and established themselves with a new Cross elsewhere. But the old sacred separatist society never came back into existence. There was no longer a real need or a real motive. On the contrary, between 1915 and the great crash of the twenties, the Maya of Quintana Roo made a relatively comfortable living on the chicle which was taken from their jungle to make chewing gum for Americans.

Chan Santa Cruz is now Felipe Carillo Puerto, but there are still *Cruzob* in the jungle. Reed, in his last chapter, speaks of visiting one of their leaders. When he had finally gained the man's confidence and convinced him of an authentic interest in the *Cruzob*, the man got a knowing look and started to talk business: What about some guns? "I had gone looking for recollections of the Caste War," Reed remarks, "and now I was invited to enlist."

6

Some reflections and conclusions. The rebellion of the Maya *Cruzob* is a paradigm of literally thousands of sectarian eschatalogical movements which spring up spontaneously and independently everywhere today. As a matter of fact, such movements have been characteristic of the Western world since the Middle Ages, but in our own time their multiplication is both universal and extraordinary. From the Cargo cults of Melanesia and Polynesia to the nativistic sectarian churches of the Bantu Prophets in South Africa to the Black Muslims and the Black Power movement in the United States and even, in some sense, to the Cultural Revolution in Red China and to Zionist Israel we see the spread of militant eschatology in one form or other, now religious, now revolutionary, now fanatically conservative, but always radical. In every case the phenomenon is one of crisis and adaptation: an effort of a minority to interpret, to evaluate and to implement its own struggle for survival in a radically new and threatening situation. There is always a definite break either with the past or with established power or with an encroaching alien intruder. There is a regrouping around an ideological or religious center. There is a display of militancy and of force. There is an aggressive affirmation of identity and of certain basic demands. The symbols and expressions of power may take forms that seem fantastic and illogical, but if we look behind them we usually find real problems and genuine grievances which cannot be dealt with by existing political or cultural means.

The fifty year life span of the segregated and sacred society of the Mayan "Cross-people" would seem to be about normal for a radical and sectarian minority movement of this kind. The intense feelings of revolt and separatism, nourished by voices and miracles, cannot be sustained much longer than this: but the revolutionary fervor of the beginnings can always subside and give place to a working political existence in which things settle down and become "normal." This means of course that relations with the rest of the world are also normal. The complete isolation of the *Cruzob* from the rest of the world—an isolation which maintained their zeal and on which they built their hope of survival—was in fact their ruin.

With a deeper fund of experience, of political knowledge and of international awareness, it is conceivable that the Mayans could have taken over Yucatán and run it as an Indian nation—especially if they had received aid from outside. That was out of the question a hundred years ago. But today, with revolutionary groups in all parts of the world becoming more conscious of each other's existence and even able to some extent to help one another, the situation is different. However, many other factors enter into the picture to complicate it: technology, world revolutionary movements, modern warfare, cultural and economic explosion and the widening gulf of bewilderment even among those who think they are in control: all this makes it unlikely that a few "pure" sects might aid one another in isolated and "sacred" self-affirmation. The complexity of all these factors, nevertheless, seems to guarantee that there will be many more such scattered movements of apocalypse and resistance in our time.

THE SACRED CITY

T HE VALLEY OF OAXACA is one of the poorest and least productive areas of Mexico today. It was once one of the
richest and most fertile. It was also the center not only of a
great culture, but of what was probably the first real city in
America: Monte Albán. What was this city? What kind of
culture flourished there? What kind of people lived there?

Archaeological studies* have now brought to light some
very rich and detailed material concerning the "early urban"
and "pre-classic" Zapotecan culture of the Oaxaca valley and
its central city. We are finally in a position to fit Monte Albán
into the general picture of Mesoamerican civilization of the
"classic" age, before the rise of the Mixtecs, Toltecs and Aztecs whose culture was essentially decadent.

Before we even begin to speak of Monte Albán and of the
ancient Mayan cities which had much in common with it, we
must put out of our minds the generalized idea of ancient cities
which we have associated with Egypt and Mesopotamia, or
with our sketchy knowledge of post-classic Mexican (Toltec
and Aztec) culture in the five centuries preceding the Spanish

---

*This essay is essentially an appreciation of a new collection of studies—
reports on "Discoveries in Mexican Archaeology and History" edited by
John Paddock under the title *Ancient Oaxaca,* and published by the
Stanford University Press, 1966. It contains two very important surveys,
"Mesoamerica before the Toltecs" by Wigberto Jiménez Moreno, and
"Oaxaca in Ancient Mesoamerica" by John Paddock. Eight other shorter
papers by archaeologists, Alfonso Caso, Ignacio Bernal, and other scholars,
are mainly concerned with the relations of the Zapotec and Mixtec cultures after the "Classic" period. The two longer studies are essential for a
contemporary evaluation of Zapotec culture in its relation to the other
civilizations of Middle America.
We also refer to the new edition of the standard work of Sylvanus Morley,
The Ancient Maya, revised by George W. Brainerd, 3rd edition, Stanford,
1956.

conquest. In these ancient cultures which are more familiar to us the city stands out as the stronghold of a monarch or tyrant, a potential empire builder with an army and a culture based upon slavery. The City, in other words, comes into being with kingship or at least with militaristic autocracy, and urban culture is a culture not only of commerce but above all of war and conquest. True, the less well known archaic cultures of the Cretans and Etruscans seem to have been less warlike, but they were also more isolated.

The popular estimate of Mexican and Mayan culture, based primarily on the reports of the Spanish conquerors and on their observations at the time of the conquest, gives us an idea of a very colorful but also bloodthirsty and necrophilic city life in which war, slavery and human sacrifice play a dominant part.* In a word, when we think of the first cities we instinctively think also of "war," "power," "wealth," "autocracy," "empire," and so on. Possible exceptions (such as Jerusalem, the "city of peace") are ambivalent enough to be no exceptions. But the first cities in America were not like Nineveh, Babylon, Ur or Thebes—or Rome. The western "ideal" city has always of course been Athens the independent, the democratic, the sophisticated. Could Monte Albán or Tikal be compared with Athens? Not really, except in so far as they were highly aesthetic cultures and seem to have been in a certain sense "democratic," though perhaps not in a way that fits our own familiar humanist rationalistic and western concept of democracy.

The most recent studies of Mesoamerican culture enable us to reconstruct a general picture of man and civilization on our continent, and in order to situate Monte Albán correctly, it might be well to look first at the general picture. This will help correct the foreshortening of perspectives in the popular view of Mexico.

We now know that hunters of mammoth were established

---

*This view of American Indian civilization is typically repeated in the Time-Life Book on Ancient America by Jonathan Norton Leonard, *Great Ages of Man,* N. Y. 1967.

in the Valley of Mexico as far back as 12,000 B.C.—when the continental ice sheet came as far south as the Ohio River and Mexico had a cool, rainy climate. With the extinction of the big game a new kind of culture developed. Agriculture seems to have been introduced after 7000 B.C. with the rudimentary cultivation of squash and then eventually of maize. It is of course on maize culture that the whole Mesoamerican Indian civilization is built.

Where was maize first grown? For a long time the highlands of Guatemala were thought to be the place where corn was originally cultivated. Recently, discoveries in a dry area of northern Oaxaca have given us a complete sequence of ancient remains of maize in its evolution from a wild to a domesticated plant. This domestication certainly goes back beyond 4000 B.C. At any rate, for a thousand years or more there flourished a neolithic, maize growing, semi-nomad, pre-ceramic culture in Mexico. Ceramics began to be made around 3000 B.C. and of course the ceramic art became one of the most highly developed and sophisticated of the Indian civilization. Metal tools were known about 1000 B.C. but never entirely supplanted stone implements which continued in use down to the Spanish conquest. Thus we have some two millenia and more of neolithic village life before the appearance of a city in Mexico. How does the Mesoamerican city develop? It is not primarily the result of a population explosion. The first city develops as a cult center, and about the year 1000 we find evidence of such centers among the Olmecs in the jungle lowlands of Vera Cruz. Many of the Mayan cities were merely centers of worship, sometimes uninhabited except by a small population of priests and scholars occupied with the important social task of determining the proper dates for clearing, planting, etc. as well as fortunate and unfortunate days for various activities. For the authentic urban center, what is required is a moderate concentration of population and of economic activity, a development of science that includes the knowledge of writing and of chronology—and of course astronomy and mathematics. And one also seeks evidence of planning, as well as of permanent monumental public buildings: evidence in other words of a relatively advanced culture, prosperous and creative, which at the same time stimulates and satisfies the higher aesthetic and intellectual needs of the community. This appears for the first time in Monte Albán, several hundred years before the construction of the Maya cities of Guatemala.

The city of Monte Albán was built somewhere between 1000 and 500 B.C. by Zapotecan Indians who knew writing, had a calendar, were astronomers and were probably the first city dwellers in America. Pottery finds at Monte Albán have brought to light an archaic style, examples of which go back to about 800 B.C. But with the paving of the Great Plaza after 300 B.C. we definitely enter upon the great period of urban culture at Monte Albán. There is a certain amount of complexity in the terms used by scholars, due to the fact that the word "Classic" has become ambiguous. Morley used it to designate the Mayan culture of the 4th to 10th centuries A.D. It was until recently assumed that the Mexican and Mayan urban cultures were all roughly contemporaneous and "Classic" was used loosely of any urban culture. Attempts to find a more accurate classification have resulted in complex charts and correlations, with Pre-Classic, Classic and Post-Classic or Epi-classic, broken up into numerous subdivisions, and reaching out to include the widely different cultures of Guatemala, Yucatán, Vera Cruz, Mexico, Oaxaca, etc. These charts may be very illuminating to the experts, but to the general reader they are not much help.

To put it in the simplest terms, we can lump together everything from 1000 B.C. to 900 A.D. as "Classic" or "Early" (though it includes various degrees because about 900 A.D. Monte Albán was abandoned and so were the "Classic" Maya cities like Petén, Uaxactun and other centers in Guatemala). After this time, the Mayan culture spread out in Yucatán in a Post-Classical civilization under Toltec domination, and in the Oaxaca Valley the old Zapotec society yielded to Mixtec conquerors who occupied fortified towns of the region like Mitla and Yagul. The six hundred year period between 900

A.D. and the Spanish conquest can be called "Post-Classical" or "Late." Note that by the time the Spaniards arrived, even the last, post-classic Mayan cities of Yucatán had been abandoned. Mayan urban civilization was at an end. But the Aztecs had a flourishing city of three hundred thousand at Tenochitlán (on the site of Mexico City).

The great difference between the two cultures and the two periods is this. In the early or Classical cultures there is almost no evidence of militarism, of war, or of human sacrifice until very late. The late, Post-Classical civilization results from the radical change from a peaceful to a warlike and militaristic way of life brought in by conquering and relatively barbarous tribes from the north. The Mixtecs conquered the Zapotecs who had abandoned Monte Albán (though still sporadically worshipping there). The Toltecs overcame the Mayas and produced a hybrid Toltec-Mayan culture in Yucatán, centered especially in Chichen Itza. It is with the "late" period that history really begins. The history of the Oaxaca Valley starts with important Mixtec codices—such as the famous Bodley Codex 14-IV-V which tells the story of the Cacique called "Eight Deer Tiger Claw" who ends up being sacrificed. Alfonso Caso's study in Paddock shows that the value of these Mixtec codices is greatly enhanced by recent discoveries in tombs of the Oaxaca valley.

But in the Classic period there are no chronicles. Even though there are many dated stelae in classic Mayan architecture and at Monte Albán, the "dates" are at first non-historical. They refer to cosmic cycles, to the stars, and to events that may be called "divine" rather than historical. In other words the Classic chronologists were more concerned with cosmic happenings than with the rise and fall of kings and empires, with gods rather than with kings. Not that this concern with the gods excluded care for human existence: for by liturgy and celebration, the lives of men, cultivators of maize, were integrated in the cosmic movements of the stars, the planets, the skies, the winds and weather, the comings and goings of the gods. That this society was not dominated by what Marx called religious alienation is evident from the fact that its art did not represent the gods until very late: the early art represents the people themselves, the celebrants officiating in liturgical rites and feasts, vested in the splendid and symbolic emblems of their totem.

We are only just beginning to realize the extraordinary sophistication of totemic thought (as interpreted by Claude Lévi-Strauss). Living records left by such North American Indians as Black Elk and Two Leggings suggest that the elaborate symbolic association of the human person with cosmic animals represents something much more intimate than an "alienated" subjection to external forces. We know something of the profoundly interior relationship of the North American hunter with his "vision power," and we know that the Central American Indian remained in extremely close relationship with the divinity that ruled the day of his birth and gave him one of his names. What we have here is in fact not a matter of alienation of identity—but it is obviously a conception of identity which is quite different from our subjective and psychological one, centered on the empirical ego regarded as distinct and separate from the rest of reality.

This "objective" identity seems to have been fully integrated into a cosmic system which was at once perfectly sacred and perfectly worldly. There is no question that the Indian in the "sacred city" felt himself completely at home in his world and perfectly understood his right place in it. And this is what we are to understand, apparently, by the splendor and symbolism of an art which signified that the gods were present not in idols or sanctuaries so much as in the worshipper, his community and his world. The individual found himself, by his "objective" identity, at the intersection of culture and nature, crossroads established by the gods, points of communication not only between the visible and the invisible, the obvious and the unexplained, the higher and lower, the strong and the helpless: but above all between complementary opposites which balanced and fulfilled each other (fire-water, heat-cold, rain-earth, light-dark, life-death). "Self-realization" in such a context implied not so much the ego-consciousness of the isolated subject in the face of a multitude of objects, but the awareness of a network of relationships in which one had a place in the mesh. One's identity was the intersection of cords where one "belonged." The intersection was to be sought in terms of a kind of musical or aesthetic and scientific synchronicity—one fell in step with the dance of the universe, the liturgy of the stars.

What kind of life was led in the "Classic" cities of Guatemala or Oaxaca? We can say that for roughly two thousand years the Zapotecan and Mayan Indians maintained an entirely peaceful, prosperous civilization that was essentially aesthetic and religious. This civilization was focussed in urban cult-centers, but it was not what we could call a truly urban culture.

Although it has been maintained that Tikal once had a population of 100,000, the Maya cities were usually quite small—and indeed had few permanent residents apart from the priests and scholars who served the temples and observatories. Most of the population was more or less rural, living outside amid the cornfields (*milpas* or *col*) which were periodically cleared from the jungle and then allowed to run wild again. Since there was no war, at least on any scale larger than perhaps family or tribal feuding, there was no need to concentrate the population within fortified towns—until, of course, in the Post-Classical period. It was perfectly safe for families, clans and other small groups to live in jungle villages as they had done from time immemorial. The city was where they came together for special celebration, for the worship which included the games and dances in which they took intense satisfaction and gained a heightened awareness of themselves as individuals and as a society. This worship was also completely integrated in their seasonal round of clearing the *milpa,* burning brush, planting, cultivating and harvesting the maize. This work did not take up an exorbitant amount of time, and in the great periods of enthusiasm and prosperity the people gave their surplus time and energy to the common construction projects which some of the modern scholars still find hard to understand. The example of Egypt and Assyria would suggest slave labor, yet all the evidence seems to indicate that the Mayans and Zapotecans built their classic cities spontaneously, freely, as a communal expression of solidarity, self-awareness, and aesthetic and religious creativity. There is no evidence of slavery until the Post-Classical period.

The success of these two thousand years of peaceful, creative existence, demanded a well-developed sense of coordination, a division of tasks under the direction of specialists, a relatively high proportion of skilled labor, and above all a completely unanimous acceptance of a common vision and attitude toward life. One must of course avoid the temptation to idealize what was still in many respects a Stone Age culture, but one cannot evade the conviction that these must have been very happy people. The Mayan scholar, Morley, quotes an English statesman who said "the measure of civilization is the extent of man's obedience to the unenforceable" and comments that by this standard the Mayans must have measured high. John Paddock, writing of the Zapotecs of Monte Albán, and remarking that there is no evidence of slavery there, says:

> No whip-cracking slave driver was needed. The satisfaction of helping to create something simultaneously imposing, reassuring and beautiful is enough to mobilize endless amounts of human effort.

He goes on to argue from the persistence of pilgrimage and generosity in the Mexican Indian of today:

> It is common for tens of thousands of men, women and children to walk 50 or more miles to a shrine. They are not slaves; they would revolt if denied the right to make their pilgrimage . . . Mexico's shrines of today are in most cases far less beautiful and the worshiper's participation (with money) is far less satisfyingly direct; but they still come by the thousands voluntarily.

What Paddock is trying to explain here is not merely the fact that a religious center, a "sacred city" like Monte Albán existed, but that it was in fact built on a mountain ridge, without the use of wheels for transport and without draft animals —as also without slave labor. The fantastically difficult work was carried out with immense patience and love by people whose motives cannot even be guessed, if we try to analyze them solely in economic or technological terms.

Here was a major religious capital, an urban complex which at the height of its prosperity "occupied not only the top of a large mountain but the tops and sides of a whole range of high hills adjoining, a total of some fifteen square miles of urban construction" (Paddock). The maintenance of the city "would necessarily require the services of thousands of specialists: priests, artists, architects, the apprentices of all these and many kinds of workmen, including servants for the dignitaries and their families." The peaceful and continuous growth of this city and its culture—with continued renewal of buildings and art work century after century—can only be explained by the fact that the people liked it that way. They wanted to build new temples and to dance in the Great Plaza dressed in their beautiful costumes. Nor were they particularly anxious to find quicker and more efficient methods of doing their work. They were in no hurry. An artist was content to grind for months on a jade pebble to carve out a glyph. And he was not even paid for it!

> In purely economic terms, in fact, the whole accomplishment seems fantastic. But if we attempt to comprehend it in economic terms alone we are neglecting the crucial factors. For over a century we have been living in a world where technology has been the great hope, solving one problem after another. Perhaps we may be forgiven if we have come to demand material-mechanical explanations for everything, overlooking the possibility that they may often be insufficient . . . . To ask these questions only in economic, technological or political terms will produce only some of the needed answers. Questions about religion and art must be included, and they may be in this case the most basic ones.
>
> *Paddock*

The chief economic factor in the success of the Zapotec civilization was that in the fertile, isolated Oaxaca valley, a relatively small population, which remained stable, had a highly effective system for exploiting the natural advantages of their region. They could produce the food they needed—plenty of corn, squash, tomatoes, peppers, avocados, red and black beans, cacao, along with tobacco and cotton. They engaged in some commerce with the so called "Olmec" civilization in the jungle lowlands of what is now the state of Vera Cruz, and later with the people in the Valley of Mexico to the north. But their surplus time and energy went into art, architecture and worship. The result was a city and a culture of great majesty and refinement, integrated into a natural setting of extraordinary beauty, dominating the fertile valley surrounded by high mountains. The people who collaborated in the work and worship of the sacred city must have enjoyed a most unusual sense of communal identity and achievement. Wherever they looked, they found nothing to equal their creative success which antedated that of the Classic Mayan culture by more than five hundred years, and was not outshone by the latter when it finally dawned.

The archaeology of the Oaxaca Valley is still only in its first stages, and further discoveries will bring to light much more that has been barely guessed at so far. But we know enough accurately to surmise what it was all about. Paddock says:

> Monte Albán was a place electric with the presence of the gods. These gods were the very forces of nature with which peasants are respectfully intimate . . .
> Every temple stood over a half a dozen temples of centuries before. Buried in the great temples were ancient high priests of legendary powers, now semi-deified; centuries of accumulated wealth in offerings, centuries of mana in ceremonies, centuries of power and success, lay deep inside that masonry. But with their own humble hands, or those of their remembered ancestors, the common people had made the buildings . . . They were participating in the life of the metropolis; they could see that they were making it possible. They could stand dazzled before those mighty temples, stroll half an hour to circle the immense open plaza, watch the stunning pageantry of the ceremonies, stare as fascinated as we at the valley spread out mile after mile below. They knew that no other such center existed for hundreds of miles—and even then their city had only rivals, not superiors . . .

Three things above all distinguish this "sacred city" from our own culture today: the indifference to technological progress, the lack of history, and the almost total neglect of the arts of war. The three things go together, and are rooted in an entirely different conception of man and of life. That conception, of which we have already spoken as a network of living interrelationships, can be called synthetic and synchronic, instead of analytic and diachronic.

In plain and colloquial terms it is a difference between a peaceful, timeless life lived in the stability of a continually renewed present, and a dynamic, aggressive life aimed at the future. We are more and more acutely conscious of travelling, of going somewhere, of heading for some ultimate goal. They were conscious of having arrived, of being at the heart of things. Mircea Eliade speaks of the archaic concept of the sanctuary or the sacred place as the *axis mundi,* the center or navel of the earth, for those whose lives revolve in the cycles of its liturgy.

Perhaps the inhabitants of these first American cities, who remained content in large measure with stone age techniques, who had no sense of history—and certainly no foresight into what was to come after their time!—simply accepted themselves as having more or less unconsciously achieved the kind of successful balance that humanity had been striving for, slowly and organically, over ten thousand and more years. Their material needs were satisfied and their life could expand in creative self-expression. This was the final perfection of the long, relatively peaceful agrarian society that had grown out of the neolithic age.

According to our way of thinking, the Zapotecs were crazy not to make use of the wheel when they knew of its existence. The curious thing is that they had wheels, but only for toys. And they did use rollers to move heavy blocks of stone. They were in a word perfectly capable of "inventing the wheel" but for some reason (which must remain to us profoundly mysterious) they never bothered with it. They were not interested in going places.

The Indian cultures of Mesoamerica are typical archaic societies in which the creative energy of the people found expression in artistic and religious forms rather than in applied science. This is, to us, one of the most baffling of problems. Greco-Roman civilization—which was much more pragmatic and practical than that of the Indians—also presents this problem. The science of the Alexandrian scholars in the Roman empire was sufficiently advanced to permit the development of steam engines. The industrial revolution might have taken place in 200 A.D. But it didn't. So might the discovery of America, for that matter, as the Alexandrian geographers were aware that the earth was round.

What is most perplexing to us is that, as a matter of fact, economic conditions called for this kind of development. To our way of thinking, the Zapotecs needed wheels and machinery, and the economy of the late Roman empire demanded a technological revolution. Just as the Mesoamerican Indians used wheels only for toys, so the Romans also used hydraulic power, but only for shifting heavy scenery in the Circus.

A few modern scholars have tried to grapple with this enigma, and Hanns Sachs, a psychoanalyst, contends that the urge for technological progress was suppressed in the ancient world because of the radically different disposition of narcissism and libido in ancient man. Tools and machines replace the body and absorb or alienate libido energy which is frankly cathected by sensuous man.

Once again we come upon the curious question of archaic man's *sense of identity*. His sense of his own reality and actuality was much more frankly bound up with sensual experience and body narcissism, whereas we have been split up and tend to project our libido outward into works, possessions, implements, money, etc. In the lovely sculptured *danzantes* (dancers) of Monte Albán, with their frank and sensuously flowering male nakedness, we apprehend a bodily awareness that substantiates what Sachs says: "To these men of antiquity the body, which they could cathect with a libido still undeviated, was their real being . . . . Animistic man vitalized the inanimate world with such narcissism as he could find no other use for."

The "reality" and "identity" of archaic man was then centered in sensuous self-awareness and identification with a close, ever-present and keenly sensed world of nature: for us, our "self" tends to be "realized" in a much more shadowy, abstract, mental world, or indeed in a very abstract and spiritualized world of "soul." We are disembodied minds seeking to bridge the gap between mind and body and return to ourselves through the mediation of things, commodities, products and implements. We reinforce our sense of reality by acting on the external world to get ever new results. More sensuous, primitive man does not understand this and recoils from it striving to influence external reality by magic and sensuous self-identification.

The primitive, like the child, remains in direct sensuous contact with what is outside him, and is most happy when this contact is celebrated in an aesthetic and ritual joy. He relates to things and persons around him with narcissistic play. Our narcissism has been increasingly invested, through intellectual operations, in the money, the machine, the weaponry, which are the extensions of ourselves and which we venerate in our rituals of work, war, production, domination and brute power.

Obviously the Zapotecs of Monte Albán knew what violence was. They knew what it meant to fight and kill: they were not a "pacifist society" (which would imply a conscious and programmatic refusal of war). They just had no use for war, as a community. It was pointless. They were not threatened, and it evidently did not enter their heads to threaten others— until the far end of the classic period when a growing population had exhausted the reserves of land, when the deforested mountains were eroded and the hungry, restless community began to look for places to plant corn in the territory of others —or to fight others who came looking for more room in Oaxaca.

By this time, of course, the long centuries of high classic civilization were coming to an end everywhere in Mexico and Yucatán. Already in the seventh century A.D. the metropolis of the Valley of Mexico, Teotihuacán, had been sacked or burned. In the tenth century, Monte Albán was deserted. But it was never conquered and indeed never attacked. There were never any fortifications— and indeed there was never a need for any. There is no evidence of violent, revolutionary destruction—the city was not harmed. It just came to an end. The enterprise of sacred culture closed down. Its creativity was exhausted.

There is no satisfactory explanation as yet of why the classic sacred cities of the Mayans and Zapotecs were simply abandoned. Presumably the ancient civilization finally grew too rigid and died of sclerosis. Its creative and self-renewing power finally gave out. Sometimes it is assumed that the people became disillusioned with the ruling caste of priests and revolted against them. But we also hear of a migration of priests and scholars into the south, under pressure of invasion from the north. In any case the cities were abandoned.

The Zapotecs were conquered by their neighbors the Mixtecs after Monte Albán was abandoned, but they continued to live under their conquerors, maintaining, it is said, a "government in exile" somewhere else. Today, the Zapotecs persist, their language is still spoken, and in their ancestral territory they have outlasted the Mixtecs who remain in a minority.

The Spanish conquered Mesoamerica in the sixteenth century. The blood-thirsty Aztec empire, built on military power, ruled Mexico. But it was hated and decadent. It was willingly betrayed by the other Indians and collapsed before the guns of Christian Spain. Much of the ancient Indian culture was destroyed, above all, anything that had to do with religion. But we must remember that the finest Mesoamerican civilizations had already disappeared seven or eight hundred years before the arrival of the Europeans.

After the conquest, the Oaxaca valley, once rich and fertile, gradually became a near-desert as the ancient agricultural practices were forgotten and the soil of the deforested mountains washed out. Contact with the Europeans was in many ways a human disaster for the Mexicans. The Indian population of Mesoamerica was probably twenty million in 1519. In 1532 it was already under seventeen million, in 1550 it was down to six million and in 1600 there were *only a million Indians left*. The population dropped nineteen million in eighty years. This was not due to systematic genocide but to diseases which the Indians could not resist. The impact of Spain on Mexico was in effect genocidal. Fortunately, a slow recovery began in the mid seventeenth century.

To summarize: the extraordinary thing about the Zapotec civilization of the Oaxaca Valley is that, like the Classic urban civilization of the Mayas and the so-called "Olmec" or Tenocelome culture, it maintained itself without war and without military power for many centuries. We can say that Monte Albán, in its pre-urban as well as in its urban development, represents a peaceful and prosperous culture extending over two millenia without a full scale war and without any need of fortifications or a defense establishment.

In the present state of our knowledge of Zapotec culture, we can say that for two thousand years Monte Albán had no history but that of its arts and its creative achievement. Indeed, the only chronology we have is determined by different styles in ceramics, architecture and sculpture. We may hope that further archaeological finds and a better understanding of hieroglyphic writing may give us an idea of the development of scientific, philosophical and religious thought in Monte Albán. But we have here an almost unique example of a city state whose history is entirely creative, totally centered in artistic work, in thought, in majestic ritual celebration. We may add that it is intensely and warmly human and often marked with a very special charm, humor, and taste. Even in its baroque stage, Zapotec Classic art is less bizarre than Mayan, and of course it never approaches the necrophilic bad taste of the Aztecs.

A more detailed knowledge of the religious thought and development of the people at Monte Albán may perhaps show us a gradual change, with an archaic, totemistic, ancestor-plus-fertility religion and a few "high gods," giving place eventually to a more and more hierarchical religious establishment, an increasingly complex theogony and a whole elaborate pantheon of deified nature forces and culture heroes to be bought off by sacrifice.

In other words, it may be that at Monte Albán and in the ancient Maya cities we may witness the gradual transition from neolithic village-agrarian culture to the warlike imperial metropolis, through the theocratic establishment of urban power in the hands of priest-kings. But it appears from the recent studies that life in the classic era of Monte Albán was still "democratic" not in the sophisticated sense of the Greek *polis* but in the archaic sense of the neolithic village. It was a life of creative common participation in the general enterprise of running the sacred city as a permanent celebration.

This was made possible by special circumstances: a fertile and productive region, not too thickly populated, which allowed all the material needs of the people to be satisfied with a small amount of field work, and liberated the surplus energies for common urban projects in art and architecture, as well as for religious celebration. The energy and wealth that other cultures put into wars of conquest, the Zapotecs simply put into beautifying and ennobling their common agrarian and city life. But of course they did this entirely without self-consciousness, and their art, unlike ours, was spontaneously and completely integrated in their everyday lives. They did not take courses in art appreciation or go dutifully to the opera, or seek out good paintings in a museum.

Since this kind of life was impossible except in a small and isolated population, it flourished under conditions which have become practically unthinkable in our present day world. We have to look for some other formula. Nevertheless, it will not hurt us to remember that this kind of thing was once possible, indeed normal, and not a mere matter of idealistic fantasy.

The Chinese sage, Lao Tse, writing at the time when the first temples were being built on the hilltops at Monte Albán, described his ideal state in these terms:

> A small country with a small population
> Where the supply of goods is ten or a hundred times
> more than they can use,
> Let people value their lives and not travel far
> Though there be boats and carriages
> No one there to ride in them
> Though there be arms and weapons
> No need to brandish them.
> Let them count with a knotted string
> Enjoy their food
> Wear beautiful clothes
> Be satisfied with their houses
> Delight in their customs
> You can see from one town to the other
> You can hear the dogs barking and cocks crowing
> In the other village
> And you can live your whole life without going
> over from one to the other.

Lao Tse might have been describing the life-tempo and the prevailing attitudes in the Oaxaca valley, among people whose remote ancestors had come, thousands of years before, from Asia.

By way of summary and conclusion: the purpose of this study is not merely to draw an unfavorable contrast between the peaceful, stable, aesthetic existence of the "sacred city," and the turbulent, unstable and vulgar affluence of the warfare state—the "secular city." To say that Monte Albán was nice and that New York is ghastly would be an irrelevant exercise, especially since the writer likes New York well enough and does not think of it as ghastly—only as a place where he is well-content to be no longer a resident. It is all too easy for people who live, as we do, in crisis, to sigh with nostalgia for a society that was once so obviously tranquil and secure. Yet there is some advantage in remembering that after all peace, tranquillity and security were once not only possible but real. It is above all salutary for us to realize that they were possible only on terms quite other than those which we take for granted as normal.

In other words, it is important that we fit the two thousand war-less years of Monte Albán into our world-view. It may help to tone down a little of our aggressive, self-complacent superiority, and puncture some of our more disastrous myths. The greatest of these is doubtless that we are the first civilization that has appeared on the face of the earth (Greece was all right in so far as it foreshadowed the U.S.A.). And the corollary to do this: that all other civilizations, and particularly those of "colored" races, were always quaintly inferior, mere curious forms of barbarism. We are far too convinced of many other myths about peace and war, about time and history, about the inherent purpose of civilization, of science, of technology and of social life itself, and these illusions do us no good. They might be partly corrected by a sober view of the undoubted success achieved by the Zapotec Indians.

The "sacred cities" of Monte Albán and of Guatemala, as we see them, looked back rather than forward. They were the fulfillment of a long development of a certain type of culture which was agrarian and which flourished in small populations. With the growth of populous societies, the accumulation of wealth, the development of complex political and religious establishments and above all with the expansion of invention and resources for war, human life on earth was revolutionized. That revolution began with what we call "history" and has reached its climax now in another and far greater revolution which may, in one way or other, bring us to the end of history. Will we reach that end in cataclysmic destruction or—as others affably promise—in a "new tribalism," a submersion of history in the vast unified complex of mass-mediated relationships which will make the entire world one homogeneous city? Will this be the purely secular, technological city, in which all relationships will be cultural and nature will have been absorbed in techniques? Will this usher in the millenium? Or will it be nothing more than the laborious institution of a new kind of jungle, the electronic labyrinth, in which tribes will hunt heads among the aerials and fire escapes until somehow an eschatological culture of peace emerges somewhere in the turbulent structure of artifice, abstraction and violence which has become man's second nature?

Inevitably, such a culture will have to recover at least something of the values and attitudes that were characteristics of Monte Albán.

UNICORN KEEPSAKE SERIES
Modern Classics of poetry, prose & visual arts

VOLUME 1
VIETNAM POEMS
Nhat Hanh
Translated by the author & Helen Coutant

VOLUME 2
SEVEN POEMS
Boris Pasternak
Translated by George L. Kline

VOLUME 3
TREE OF SONG
Federico García Lorca
Translated by Alan Brilliant

VOLUME 4
TWELVE PHOTOGRAPHIC PORTRAITS
John Howard Griffin

VOLUME 5
THE JAGUAR & THE MOON
Pablo Antonio Cuadra
Translated by Thomas Merton

VOLUME 6
SONGS OF MRIRIDA:
Courtesan of the High Atlas
Translated by Daniel Halpern & Paula Paley

VOLUME 7
VIETNAMESE FOLK POETRY
Transcribed & Translated by John Balaban
Woodcut by Vo-Dinh

VOLUME 8
ISHI MEANS MAN
Essays on Native Americans
Thomas Merton

VOLUME 9
GOOD MESSAGE OF HANDSOME LAKE
Joseph Bruchac